CANADA'S BIG HOUSE

This book is dedicated to the memory of my paternal ancestor,
James Hennessy of Ameliasburg, 1796–c.1860.

CANADA'S BIG HOUSE

THE DARK HISTORY OF THE KINGSTON PENITENTIARY

PETER H. HENNESSY

THE DUNDURN GROUP
TORONTO · OXFORD

Editor: Kathy Lim
Design: Scott Reid
Printer: Transcontinental Printing Inc.

Canadian Cataloguing in Publication Data

Hennessy, Peter H., 1927–
Canada's big house: the dark history of the Kingston Penitentiary
Includes bibliographical references.

ISBN 1-55002-330-6
1. Kingston Penitentiary — History. I. Title.
HV9508.K56H46 1999   365'.971372   C99-932270-2

1   2   3   4   5   03   02   01   00   99

THE CANADA COUNCIL | LE CONSEIL DES ARTS
FOR THE ARTS | DU CANADA
SINCE 1957 | DEPUIS 1957

We acknowledge the support of the **Canada Council for the Arts** for our publishing program. We also acknowledge the support of the **Ontario Arts Council** and we acknowledge the financial support of the Government of Canada through the **Book Publishing Industry Development Program** (BPIDP) for our publishing activities.

Printed and bound in Canada.

Printed on recycled paper.

Dundurn Press
8 Market Street
Suite 200
Toronto, Ontario, Canada
M5E 1M6

Dundurn Press
73 Lime Walk
Headington, Oxford,
England
OX3 7AD

Dundurn Press
2250 Military Road
Tonawanda NY
U.S.A. 14150

Contents

ACKNOWLEDGMENTS

There are many people to thank for their help in producing Canada's Big House. Serving on the board of directors of the John Howard Society of Kingston since 1985 has been a gestation period for the book. Several John Howard persons, by their example, taught me the value of looking inside our prisons rather than away from them: Graham Stewart, Barbara Hill, Jane Cobden, Gordon MacFarlane, Nicki McShane, Steve Orr, Stuart Ryan, Chris Crowder, and the late Harry Botterell, come to mind. I thank them all, and many others whose names I have overlooked.

It was Christopher Dafoe, formerly editor of *The Beaver*, a history journal based in Winnipeg, who accepted an essay I wrote about the old penitentiary and thereby planted the seed for a book. I thank him.

The Kingston Historical Society and later the Quinte Historical Society showed an interest in my research into the history of the Kingston Penitentiary. Their recognition and support fuelled my determination to produce a book that might be historically respectable. I thank them.

Then there are the librarian-archivists who made me comfortable, cheerfully spread records in front of me, and offered words of encouragement. I am thinking of the staff of the National Archives in Ottawa and of Murray Millar and David St. Onge of the Correctional Services Museum at Kingston and of George Henderson, Stewart Renfrew and Gillian Barlow at the Queen's University Archives. I have been treated like royalty on their premises.

I am grateful to two popular authors for helping me catch the atmosphere of the penitentiary in earlier times: Merilyn Simonds, author of *The Convict Lover* (1996), a work of nonfiction about the Ponsford era at K.P., and Margaret Atwood, who wrote *Alias Grace* (1996), a fictional story partly set inside the penitentiary in the 1850s.

Too late to influence the content of my book but in time to inform my thinking about prisons and jails is the splendidly researched volume by Peter Oliver, *Terror to Evil-Doers* (1998).

Among those who read portions of this text, I owe a special debt to Stuart Ryan, emeritus professor of law at Queen's, whose ninety years of accumulated wisdom is only exceeded by his kindness. It was Professor Ryan who persuaded me to join the Citizens Advisory Committee at K.P. in 1992. That appointment led to extended first-hand observation of the stresses under which prison staff do their work and prisoners do their time. I thank the wardens and their assistants who were so courteous to me and all of the prisoners who spoke freely to me. My continuing anxiety is that they may think I used them for personal gain. In self-defence, I can only say that my Irish instinct for reform needs constant gratification and that there is no better vehicle for that purpose than the Kingston Penitentiary.

I thank Marion for her patience. As the rejection letters arrived in the mail, she never betrayed the least doubt about the good effect of all that time at the keyboard.

Finally, I thank Tony Hawke, Barry Jowett, Kathy Lim, and others at Dundurn Press. All those who write know that perfection is forever elusive. Book editors have the unenviable job of saying when it's time to let it go.

Peter H. Hennessy
Elginburg, Ontario
April 1999

INTRODUCTION

A book about a prison as notorious as the Kingston Penitentiary requires an honest statement of the author's intent. There are several possibilities: is it an apologia for the managers? an assertion of the futility of imprisonment? an *exposé* of sensational events behind the walls? a contribution to the prison abolition movement? an argument for prisoners' rights? a call for sweeping reform in the criminal justice system?

The driving motivation of the author forms the bias of this or any other book for that matter. Because of the strength of emotions stirred by a study of this particular prison, an unbiased account of its history is nearly inconceivable. There are books written by ex-inmates that provoke feelings of anger and moral outrage. There are scholarly books and theses, published and unpublished, aimed at the serious student of Canadian social history. Those works exhibit varying degrees of objectivity. There are countless stories written by journalists to excite and titillate the reader for a brief moment. There are polemical tracts of a radical nature pointing towards the revolution. And, not least by any means, there are vast stores of primary sources waiting for further analysis by scholars.

This book sketches the penitentiary's 165-year history as a backdrop to recent events within the institution — events witnessed by the author. After all those years and all those formal inquiries and all those calls for reform, the old prison still suffers from confusion of purpose and faulty leadership. It is as if the burden of the past cannot be thrown aside — a viewpoint that is at the heart of this work. It is as if the doctrine of human progress is merely a myth.

The challenge, then, was to select those segments of K.P.'s history that would support the writer's objective as stated above. The outcome is a series of verbal snapshots constructed mainly from original documents, such as regulations, letters, and official prison records. These excerpts from the historical record are intended to present a coherent procession of people and events from 1835, when the first chained convicts arrived, to the end of the twentieth century.

In the outcome, much more of the history of the penitentiary is omitted than is included. Those curious about spectacular events such as the escapes of high-profile convicts Mickey McDonald and Red Ryan or the murder of prison guard John Kennedy will have to look elsewhere.

Though much attention is paid to the political structure within which the prison functioned, more is paid to the everyday living and working arrangements of the convicts. Indeed, describing the circumstances of the Kingston Penitentiary prisoner, whether now or in the distant past, is the dominant feature of the book. Out of those descriptions come some very troubling questions about our criminal justice system.

We have in Canada a sophisticated system for apprehending and trying law-breakers according to principles of fairness and decency in a democratic society. But we continue to struggle with the questions: Who should be imprisoned? and what should be done with them once imprisoned? It is hoped that this book will be a useful contribution to that debate.

CHAPTER ONE
BUILT OF LIMESTONE AND RULES

*And whereas, if many offenders, convicted of Crimes for which
Transportation* [shipment to a faraway colony] *hath been usually
inflicted, were ordered to solitary confinement, accompanied by
well-regulated Labour and religious Instruction, it might be the
means, under Providence, not only of deterring others from the
Commission of like Crimes, but also of reforming the Individuals,
and inuring them to habits of industry.*
— from the *Penitentiary Houses Act*, Great Britain, 1779.[1]

In 1833 a local committee of three recommended the
construction of a provincial jail on Hatter's Bay on the west
side of Kingston, Upper Canada. The three enjoyed sterling
reputations: Christopher Hagerman, Loyalist and judge; John
Macaulay, prosperous Kingston merchant; and Hugh Thomson,
merchant-publisher-editor and reform politician. Thomson was
the chairman and spark plug of the committee; sad to say, he died
in 1834 before his dream of a reforming prison could be realized.

These pillars of the roughneck young community
recommended a prison that would "be a place by every means
not cruel and not affecting the health of the offender, [but] shall
be rendered so irksome and so terrible that during [the convict's]

afterlife he may dread nothing so much as a repetition of the punishment..." The contradiction embedded in this initial mandate set the stage for the painful and tortuous history of the Kingston Penitentiary.

The south detention wing, the first of four, was built in 1835 on ten acres of land a mile west of the town. The site was near-perfect. It possessed a quarry of excellent limestone for the construction of the first buildings. Overlaying the rock was a mantle of clay for the gardens, yards, and fields of an institution meant to confine as many as eight hundred errant men, women, and children. Not least among its advantages, the property sloped away gently to the shores of Lake Ontario which, over time, would receive incalculable amounts of human and animal waste. On the west side was Hatter's Bay, a snug harbour for boats bearing supplies, visitors, and fresh convicts to the very doorstep of the prison.

The first Board of Inspectors to oversee the prison's daily operation comprised C.W. Grant, John Macaulay (see above), John Solomon Cartwright, Alexander Pringle, and W.H. Gray. The first warden was Henry Smith, a recent English immigrant who replaced Hugh Thomson on the Planning Committee after Thomson's untimely death. Smith was the father of a rising young lawyer and aspiring Tory politician, Henry Smith Jr., and of a younger son of uncertain prospects and unpleasant temperament, Francis (Frank) W. Smith. By the falling of the leaves in 1835 there were fifty-five convicts inside the prison, fifty-two males, and three females. The men, housed in the completed south wing, were immediately put to work constructing the other cell blocks and the wall that would confine them.

> All that we know who lie in gaol
> Is that the wall is strong;
> And that each day is like a year,
> A year whose days are long.
> — Oscar Wilde, *The Ballad of Reading Gaol*

When the statute authorizing a penitentiary in Upper Canada was passed, prisons already had a long history in the Western world.[2] The Church of Rome may have originated the concept of a jail as a place of penitence, thus the word "penitentiary." Prevented by

Christian reticence from drawing blood and committed to the principle of purification through suffering, the mediaeval church confined its wrongdoers in solitary cells. The Inquisition (not to be confused with the later Spanish Inquisition) was set up in the thirteenth century to root out heretical religious views and practices. The Inquisitors made use of prisons with cells underground that were absolutely dark inside. Many centuries later, in 1704, the new San Michele prison in papal Rome featured rows of sleeping cells, three tiers high, with a large central hall for working, eating and worshipping. The silent inmates, held by leg chains, manufactured articles for use within Vatican City.

During the reign of Queen Elizabeth I, in the late 1500s, workhouses for indigents and vagrants were opened in England on the operating principle of rigorous and routine work for the inmates. They were called "houses of correction," euphemistic terminology that persists to the present day in North American prison systems. London's Bridewell House of Correction became the model for the rest of the country. Several European states, reacting to urbanization, imitated the English in coping with their down-and-outers. Glasgow's Bridewell figured in the planning of the Canadian penitentiary.

Soon after the American Revolution, the states of Pennsylvania and New York built prisons reflecting the new penal philosophy: punishment, yes, of course, but modified by assiduous attention to the criminal's damaged soul. Influenced greatly by the ideas of the English prison reformer John Howard, the Americans seized upon the notion of silence and isolation as the means of realizing Howard's goals. Cherry Hill Penitentiary in Philadelphia featured total isolation of the prisoner as the sure and certain way to reflection, contrition, and penitence and without any risk of contamination from impure thoughts. The prisoner's cell was adjoined to a tiny workplace where, all alone, he would do assigned labour. Only persons of known virtue and skill in saving souls could visit the prisoner in his cell.

Cherry Hill, with its individualized work arrangements, was expensive and therefore not copied elsewhere. New York State opened a jail at Auburn in 1817 which, after experimentation, combined the features of solitary confinement and group work. Each range unit accommodated 240 prisoners in rows of small sleeping cells stacked five tiers high. It was hoped that the rule of silence during work hours in the prison shops combined with long hours in the cells would have the desired reforming effect on the criminal. Penitence would infiltrate the mind and heart of the lonely prisoner and Christian virtue would be the happy effect.

The Kingstonians travelled to Auburn in the early 1830s. They found the prison there altogether to their liking. Soon after, the Assembly of Upper Canada voted 12,500 pounds sterling with which to buy the land and start the construction. An American, Colonel William Powers, was brought up from Auburn to build the Canadian prison according to plans drawn by John Mills. Powers estimated the cost of construction at 56,850 pounds sterling. That might approximate 25 million dollars in the 1990s. Relying heavily on convict labour, Powers superintended the early construction whilst serving as deputy warden. He was dismissed in 1840 as a result of a developing personality conflict with Warden Smith.[3]

Security, economy, and reformation formed the triad of principles which governed the construction and management of the Provincial Penitentiary on Hatter's Bay. The widely used radial design was adopted whereby there would be four cell blocks set in the form of a cross joined together by a circular rotunda. This central hub was a practical place for close scrutiny

of prisoners both on their ranges and in their movements off-range. The "Dome," as the rotunda came to be known, became the focal point of reportings, gossip, threats, and scuttlebutt of every kind. The pulse of the prison has been registered there throughout the 165 years of its life.

Interior of the Dome, 1890. Courtesy Queen's University Archives.

The cells where the prisoners spent their long nights and all the hours of religious holidays, and where penitence was expected to occur, were like mail slots for human bodies. Stacked five storeys high and ranged in double rows the length of the wing, each cell was twenty-seven inches wide and six and two-thirds feet long. The bed, when lowered for the night, left no room to stand except at the end of the cell where the night pail was located. The entry gate to each cell was made of straps of iron interwoven to produce a lattice effect. The small window at the end of the cell was of the same material and was meant to facilitate the movement of air (though not of light) through the cell.

The arrangement of the cells was ingeniously devised to facilitate surveillance of the prisoners prone on their beds. The rear walls of the cells were separated from the outer stone wall of the cell block building by a couple of feet of open space for easy air and heat flow. Thus, the two rows of cells at each of the five tiers faced inward towards each other. The space between each row of cells was twenty feet. In the centre of that space was a walled inspection avenue three feet wide and equipped with peepholes. The avenue was elevated four feet above and below the floor level of the facing cells; thus, an official or a visitor walking the avenue could peek up or down into the cells on either side without being seen by the prisoners. The prisoners could imagine that they were being watched all the time without knowing for sure. Their cell gates opened onto narrow iron catwalks or galleries leading to stairwells down to the rotunda.

Each cell block could accommodate up to 270 inmates. The original plan called for three blocks to hold about eight hundred prisoners all together; the fourth of the cruciform, the north wing, was reserved for the few women prisoners, the senior officers, their equipment and supplies, and their families. The guards were quartered in small cottages to the north of the prison and within earshot of the bell. The penitentiary community was meant to be a model of order, discipline, hard work and upright character — exactly the qualities thought to be in short supply in the rough young colony.[4]

Upper Canada was too poor to build and operate a truly advanced penitentiary; the province was a sparsely populated frontier of British America hosting about a hundred thousand adult males in 1840 and governed by a parsimonious mother country whose enthusiasm for white colonies was fast fading. The best possible prison by the standards of the day would have provided more cell space, better qualified staff, better educational facilities, and more community involvement.

Instead, as the years went by, the prison managers were encouraged to heed the siren song of commercial profit. As early as 1850, the warden held contracts with several outside manufacturers who moved their operations right inside the prison walls and into the shop complex at the bottom of the yard. These business people had the enormous benefit of nearly free labour and of institutionally managed convict workers.

In the process, Colonel Powers' vision of keepers as "smart men, intelligent, discreet, prudent, courageous, humane, faithful, prompt, vigilant, and efficient, possessing that peculiar tact which is necessary for commanding and governing men" was soon blurred by a harsh reality: there was not enough money to recruit such paragons of virtue and accumulated merit. Even if the poorly paid keepers measured up to the angelic proportions of Colonel Powers' definition, the regimentation needed to maintain the rule of silence undermined the possibility of humane leadership. Thus, the inner contradiction of the mandate of the Provincial Penitentiary manifested itself from the beginning.

The original staff of the prison comprised a warden, deputy warden, a clerk, a chaplain, a physician-surgeon, and twenty keepers. As the prisoner population increased, the staff increased proportionally faster. The rapid growth of the place can be summarized as follows:

South Cell Block - 1834–35
North Wing (administration and female prisoners) - 1836–40
East Cell Block - 1836–45
West Cell Block - 1838–57
Kitchen and Dining Hall - 1839–41
Shop Complex (also in the radial design) - 1842–49
Hospital (adjacent to East Cell Block) - 1847–48
East Shop Annex (now the Regional Treatment Centre) - 1855–58

North Gate and Lodge - 1845
Central Rotunda and Dome - 1859–61
Warden's House - 1870–72

N

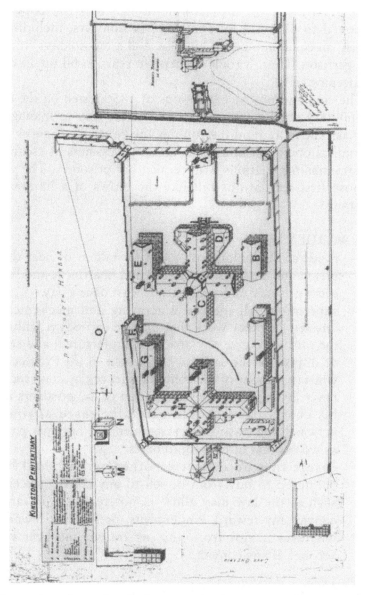

Bird's eye view of completed prison complex, late nineteenth century. Notice the tramway for horse-drawn limestone wagons stretching from the quarries north of King Street, along the east wall, looping around the south wall and through the west gate to the prison yard. Courtesy Queen's Archives.

The inmate numbers grew by leaps, paralleling the construction of the buildings. In 1842 there were 160 inmates, which included seven women and a number of military men court-martialled to imprisonment; in 1849 the total had ballooned to 475 and by 1860 to 780 convicts, including 50 women, an equal number of lunatics, and a few soldiers from the local garrison. Thus, it took twenty-five years to fill up all of the tiny sleeping cells.

The cool and precise regulations of 1836 rested on the credo that military regimentation was the correct way to manage the convicts. The more rigid the routine, the better the chances of an economical operation unmarred by such messiness as escapes or embarrassing negotiations with recalcitrant prisoners. The words of those first regulations fall like the blows of a hammer on limestone.[5]

THE WARDEN shall

— reside at the building provided for him at or near the prison and shall visit every cell and apartment and see every prisoner under his care at least once a day.

— superintend all the manufacturing and mechanical business or other work that may be carried on within the prison; receive any articles manufactured; and sell or dispose of the same to the benefit of the Province, when the labour of the convicts is let out by contract.

— never lose sight of the reformation of the prisoners in his charge, and should carefully guard against personal and passionate resentment on his own part as well as that of his subordinates.

— ensure that no officer or other person shall be permitted to buy from or sell to any convict except such as the law may allow ... nor receive from any convict any reward, emoluments, presents or reward whatever ... nor from any person whomsoever on account of any convict.

THE DEPUTY WARDEN shall

— be constantly moving about the different yards and places of labour, without previous notice, to see that every subordinate officer is vigilant and attentive to the performance of his duty, and that the convicts are vigilant, orderly and industrious.

— not allow any books, pamphlets or newspapers to be used by any of the keepers or watchmen when on duty ...

— morning, noon, and night, ascertain whether any convict is missing ...

— be present during the breakfast and dinner hours to see that the rations [for the convicts] are such as are allowed ... and that they are properly cooked and served. [see Appendix A]

DUTIES OF THE KEEPERS

As the preservation ... of the whole system of discipline depends upon the absolute prevention of intercourse [talking] among the convicts, the Keepers are to make sure ... of preventing any such intercourse or communication.

Keepers are prohibited from saying anything in the presence of convicts ... unless for the purpose of directing or instructing them in their duty.

They shall require of convicts labour, silence, and strict obedience.

They shall inflict punishment with discretion ... and in such manner and temper as may convince the offender that his conduct has rendered the punishment necessary.

They shall report daily to the Deputy Warden in writing all cases in which they have inflicted punishment ...

They must not indulge whistling, singing, scuffling, noisy conversation or laughter, or any act of insubordination or indecorum.

They must avoid conversation with each other or with the convicts, but such as is absolutely necessary in the discharge of their official duties.

They must require from the convicts great deference and respect, not suffering the least degree of familiarity to be displayed by the convicts, nor displaying any themselves.

DUTIES OF THE PHYSICIAN AND SURGEON [one person]

...every morning, he shall personally examine every sick and complaining convict ... reported by the Keepers and Overseers of the workshops ...

He shall keep a book in which shall be recorded the names of all convicts reported as sick or complaining ... and the prescriptions therefore.

He shall, from time to time, examine into the quantities of the rations, and recommend ... such changes in the diet of the convicts as he may deem necessary ... keeping in view that ... the most rigid economy is to be observed ... consistent with the health of the convict.

DUTIES OF THE CHAPLAIN

He shall furnish convicts with no intelligence other than what his profession requires.

He shall give them no hope or promise of aid in procuring pardons.

He shall be allowed free access to the convicts at all times for the purpose of imparting religious instruction and consolation.

He shall endeavour to convince the prisoners of the justice of their sentence ... and enjoin upon them strict obedience to the rules of the Penitentiary.

He shall attend every Sunday morning at 11 o'clock for the performance of Divine Service.

He shall report annually ... of the progress and state of religion amongst the convicts.

DUTIES OF THE GUARD

The Watchmen shall have no intercourse or conversation with, or control of any kind over convicts, excepting such as may be necessary to prevent their escape.

They shall keep a strict and vigilant eye upon the convicts and not suffer their attention to be for a moment diverted from their duty.

They shall suffer no person to pass to or from the prison ... without express orders.

They shall be ... under the command of the Sergeant of the Guard whose orders they shall implicitly obey.

DUTY OF CONVICTS

... all convicts shall be constantly employed at hard labour [with the necessary exceptions] except on Sundays, Christmas Day and Good Friday; it shall be the duty of the Warden to keep each prisoner singly in a cell at night and when unemployed.

... They must not exchange a word with one another under any pretence whatsoever nor communicate with one another nor with anyone else by writing.

They must not exchange looks, wink, laugh, nod, or gesticulate to each other, nor shall they make use of any signs, except as are necessary to explain their wants to the waiters...

They are not to receive from any person who does not belong to the Prison any paper, letter or tobacco or any other articles whatever ...

They are not to gaze at visitors ... passing through the Prison nor sing, dance, whistle, run, jump nor do anything which might disturb the harmony or contravene the rules of the prison.

They must not carelessly or wilfully injure their work, tools, wearing apparel, bedding or any other thing belonging to the Prison nor execute their work badly when they have the ability to do it well.

For the wilful violation of any of these duties, corporal punishment will be instantly inflicted.

The remainder of the regulations set out the daily routine of the prison in elaborate detail. For instance:

THE OPERATION OF THE NIGHT WATCH

The Keeper on duty in Keeper's Hall, having a bed provided, at nine o'clock or at such time as the Warden may prescribe, may lie down to sleep ... a small bell shall be hung near his bed attached to a wire passing through the wall so as to be accessible to the Watchmen.

SUNDAY REGULATIONS

[all prisoners locked in their cells except for chapel]

ACCESS TO THE CLOTHES ROOM
for change of clothing;

OPERATION OF THE HOSPITAL
When a convict dies, his body, if not claimed by a relative within 24 hours, shall be delivered to the Medical Society of the Midland District if any such shall be in existence.

THE KITCHEN AND WASHROOM
... convicts shall be employed in the kitchen, and washing the clothes and bedding of the convicts.

CONVICTS' RATIONS
All convicts shall be supplied with a sufficient quantity of inferior, but wholesome food. [see Appendix A]

CLEANLINESS .
.. all areas shall be swept daily ... the floors of cells shall be scrubbed frequently and the walls and ceilings whitewashed, ... the beds and bedding shall be taken out and aired once a week in the warm season and once a fortnight during the rest of the year ... if any of the bedding shall be found wilfully damaged, the offender shall be temporarily deprived of bedding.... Convicts shall not be allowed to sleep in their clothes or to lie down and rise until notice shall be given by the ringing of a bell.... In cold weather the fires shall be kept up day and night and in warm damp weather the fires shall be kept up in order to rarify the air and improve its circulation as well as to prevent the cells from damp at night.

THE FURNITURE OF THE CELLS
... a hammock as wide as the cell, and 6'3" in length, raised 18" from the floor, and two blankets and two coarse sheets ... and a strong comb. During cold weather there shall be added a straw mattress for each cell with an extra blanket.... A Bible shall also be furnished to each convict who can read.

SHOP REGULATIONS

There shall be a Keeper in each mechanical department ... Convicts shall be so arranged to have their faces seen from the inspection avenue and Keeper's desk and as far as practicable without facing each other. Convicts shall not be allowed to take a position ... as shall give the Keeper reason to believe they are holding communication but shall keep themselves so apart from each other as not to create a suspicion.... Convicts shall be shaved twice a week in their respective shops by convict barbers and their hair kept closely cropped. They shall be directed to wash their feet frequently and occasionally bathe during the warm weather.

VISITORS

Free admission at the gate each weekday [hours given] at the rate of male adults 1s.3d. and females and children at the rate of 7 1/2d.... Visitors must not be suffered to hold the least intercourse with the convicts by word, sign or gesture nor to converse among themselves or with the Officers in a tone loud enough to be heard by the convicts.

RECEPTION AND DISCHARGE OF CONVICTS

... a new convict shall be stripped of his clothing, and his person thoroughly washed and cleansed, his hair cropped and his beard shaven and prison dress put on him.... He shall be put to work according to his trade or occupation ... upon discharge the convict shall be given a decent suit of clothes taken from new convicts and such sum of money, not exceeding one pound, as the Warden may deem proper and necessary.... The Chaplain will endeavour to obtain from him a short history of his life, his parentage, education, temptations and the various steps by which he was led into a course of vice and crime ... after which he shall be discharged with suitable admonition and advice.

* * *

And never a human voice comes near
To speak a gentle word

And the eye that watches through the door
Is pitiless and hard:
And by all forgot, we rot and rot,
With soul and body marred.
    — Oscar Wilde, *The Ballad of Reading Gaol*

As the prison expanded, the regulations multiplied like weeds in an untended field. The 1836 regulations filled up nine legal-sized pages of small print. Those published under the Dominion of Canada *Penitentiary Act of 1868* filled up forty-three book-sized pages of small print. Excerpts will be cited in Chapter 4.

CHAPTER TWO
RUNNING AMOK AND THE AFTERMATH

How strong is the claim on a Christian people to see well that their prisons will not become the moral tomb of those who enter them, but schools where the ignorant are enlightened and the repentant strengthened.... We have but one penal institution of which the aim is reformation, and the little success which has as yet attended its operations, it has been our painful duty to disclose.
— Closing words of George Brown, Secretary, in the *Report upon the Conduct, Economy, Discipline and Management of the Provincial Penitentiary*, May 30, 1849.

As early as 1847 some changes were made in the regulations as a result of omission from the first set of any limits on the punishment of offenders. This serious omission had opened the floodgates of sadism, cruelty, and malevolent administration to an extent that has never been equalled since.

Warden Henry Smith treated his responsibilities seriously, especially the ones that called for strict discipline in the enforcement of silence and hard labour. Given the shabbiness of the lives of the convicts shipped to the new prison and the open-endedness of the punishment clauses in the regulations, it was entirely predictable that brutality would be the norm during

Smith's regime. For example, the fourth duty of the keepers included this sentence: "They shall punish every convict who is under their immediate direction and control for all wilful violations of discipline and duty which they may discover."

Punishments imposed on the prisoners in 1847, the peak year in the Smith spasm of cruelty, were set out in the Warden's Report[6] roughly in the order of frequency of use:

Meals of Bread and Water - 5,104 times.

The Box - 759 times. (The Box was a coffin-shaped wooden container into which the prisoner was tightly jammed; the box, with the transgressor inside, stood upright for six to nine hours; sadistic keepers sometimes poked at the prisoner with a stick through the air hole; afterwards, the released prisoner, stiff from confinement and scarcely able to walk, got himself back to his cell as best he could.)

The cats - 58 times. (The cat-o'-nine-tails was made up of a stout wooden handle with about nine long strands of knotted rawhide attached. No more than thirty-six lashes were permitted by the revised 1847 regulations except in the case of an assault on an officer for which up to fifty lashes were permitted. The prisoner, stripped to the waist, was confined for the whipping to a tall triangle of heavy hardwood placed in view of the other prisoners. With the surgeon, present, who was required to attest to the fitness of the prisoner, the keeper, with the cats in hand, approached the bound prisoner. On a signal from the surgeon, the keeper selected an unsuspecting guard nearby, handed him the cats and directed him to administer the number of strokes decreed. Frequently the skin of the prisoner broke open partway through the punishment, causing blood to ooze from the cuts. The surgeon could abort the punishment if he believed it was affecting the health of the prisoner. When it was over, the surgeon doused the cuts with an astringent powder before ordering the man to join his work gang for the rest of the day.)

Confined to Own Cell - 73 times.

Confined to Dark Cell - 69 times. (The dark cells were absolutely dark and without any furnishings or comforts whatever except for a night pail.)

The total number of punishments recorded for the year was 6,065. The report of the commission of inquiry into the affairs of the penitentiary (1849) claimed that the number of punishments recorded during Smith's years fell far short of the number actually meted out. This claim should be weighed against the fact that the guiding hand of the commission was the crusading reformer, George Brown, editor of the Toronto *Globe* and no friend of the Henry Smith family of Kingston.

The Box — A modern reproduction. Courtesy Correctional Service of Canada Museum.

With relentless vigour and straightforwardness, the report laid bare the excesses and evils of Henry Smith's rule. He was charged by the commission with incapacity, mismanagement, cruelty, falsehood, and peculation (embezzlement).[7] He was suspended from his position by the government of United Canada (the union of Upper and Lower Canada since 1841); by 1849, this government was in the hands of the Reform Party, which in turn appointed as warden a kinder and gentler man, Donald Aeneas MacDonell.

Nevertheless, Henry Smith had set in motion attitudes and practices which lasted into the twentieth century, the more so as the prison became the private preserve of keepers and guards whose sons, and their sons, often succeeded them. Working at the Pen was and still is a way of life for many Kingston families. This must partly account for the common attitude of the town that convicts are a bad lot deserving every deprivation and punishment meted out to them.

The testimony of staff, prisoners, and others, together with the comments of the commissioners, tell the story of the penitentiary during its first fourteen years. What follows are verbatim excerpts from the Brown report under headings of my devising. That within squared brackets is my occasional clarification.

PUNISHMENT OF CHILDREN

The boys and youths of a tender age are still subject to the same discipline as the more mature Convict. [One child was under 8 years of age, three were under 12, and twelve were under 16, according to the Chaplain's report of 1845]. The juvenile offender [convict Narcisse Beauche, about 15 years of age,] is yet confined with the hoary-headed evildoer. It appears that this youth got 24 corporal punishments within six months of his arrival, and all for offences either childish in their character or the evident result of [his] disordered mind. The circumstances that the lad was afflicted with a disease in the head should have secured for him, if not milder treatment, at least protection from punishment hurtful to his health, mental or bodily.

[Ex-guard Robinson, who testified before the commission,] recollects a Convict boy, named Booshee [Beauche]; he was a very small boy, 12 to 14 years of age; he was often punished very severely with the cats. His usual offence was making a noise in his cell. Recollects one night about two years ago when witness [Robinson] was on guard over the prisoners, the Prison was disturbed by this boy. He awoke in a great fright, and commenced shouting out that there was something under his bed, and calling for the Priest to come and see him. He climbed up on the rails of the window and door, screaming at the height of his lungs; blood and froth came from his mouth. Keeper Hooper went to the Warden, and calling him out of his bed; it was near midnight. When the Warden arrived, the boy was still screaming. The Warden immediately said "Open the door till I bring this scoundrel out." Hooper opened the door and at Warden's desire, witness brought Booshee out who was quite naked; the boy was laid on his back and they tried to put a gag in his mouth but did not succeed. The boy then told the Warden, in French, that he would be quiet and he was put back in his cell. Warden told witness what the boy had said. The moment the boy was put back he became as bad as ever, crying out that something was under his bed. The Warden then ordered him to be taken out of his cell again. Hooper and witness held him down and the Warden flogged him with a rope-end as long as he could stand over him. The boy was very severely cut; the stripes broke the skin. Witness's shirt received so much blood from contact with the boy that he had to change it next morning. The boy never left the cell afterwards, witness thinks, until he was declared insane and sent to the Lower Canada Lunatic Asylum in the custody of witness.

PUNISHMENT OF ADULT PRISONERS

None of the witnesses have alleged that any Convicts have been reformed by the discipline of the Prison, and the Warden has not alleged that he knows of any such.

It usually took three or four days for the back of a convict to heal after a flogging. Yet a few convicts were flogged three, four or even five times in one week.

Women too were flogged. Three were punished with the raw-hide [shaped like a jockey's whip, it was made of many strands of rawhide braided together so that it came to a point] during the two years 1844–45. "The stripes being given," wrote the Warden, "over their gowns ..." In all, eight women were flogged prior to the time of the commission of inquiry.

As many as twenty, thirty, or even forty men have been flogged in one morning, the majority of them for offences of the most trifling character.... To see crowds of full-grown men, day after day, and year after year stripped and lashed in the presence of four or five hundred persons, because they whispered to their neighbours, or lifted their eyes to the face of a passer-by, or laughed at some passing occurrence, must have obliterated from the minds of the unhappy men all perception of moral guilt, and thoroughly brutalized all their feelings.

James Brown, a violent convict, was punished till he became suicidal and was declared insane by the Surgeon. The punishment then ceased. He had received 1,002 lashes of the cats, 216 of the raw-hide plus all of the other punishments employed by the prison.

The female convict Charlotte Reveille went insane, apparently as a result of the punishments [chiefly, in her case, confinement in the Dark Cell].

The report of the commission provided a list of recorded punishments selected randomly from 1843 to 1848:

Idle and inattentive to directions - 6 cats
Threatening to knock another Convict's brains out - 24 cats
Having song books, novels, tobacco, candles, lucifers - 24 cats
Talking at work - 6 raw-hide
Giving another Convict tobacco - 24 hours Dark Cell
Making a noise in Cell, imitating bark of dog - Bread and Water
Shouting in his Cell - Box
Having tobacco - 12 cats
Refusing to work, insolent to Guard, cursing Keeper - 36 cats
    & Bread and Water
Giving blank leaf from new Bible to another Convict - 9 cats
Having two pairs of drawers on and tobacco - Box & Bread
    and Water
Taking Convict's spectacles off him and putting them on himself
    and staring about and laughing - Box and Bread and Water
Having 3 pocket handkerchiefs on person - 24 hours own cell
    and Bread and Water

CORRUPTION AND MISMANAGEMENT

What follows is my own summary of the report with verbatim excerpts in quotation marks.

Francis W. Smith, the warden's son, was dismissed as deputy sheriff of the Midland District (now east-central Ontario) "for irregular conduct." His father then appointed him kitchen steward of the penitentiary.

Guard John Watts testified before the commission that he bought "turnips from Frank Smith, three or four times, a bushel or half a bushel at a time, they were taken from the Penitentiary stores." Further, according to other testimony, Frank Smith sold prison potatoes, turnips, oatmeal, oats, bread, vinegar, and firewood to prison staff and that he supplied himself with meat and milk.

The warden owned from 150 to 200 head of poultry, as well as an ox, a cow, and hogs. A convict, whose sentence was later reduced by royal pardon, testified that he fed the warden's animals grain, potatoes, and turnips from prison supplies.

Keeper James Gleeson testified that he was dismissed, he believed, because he gave testimony against Frank Smith and because he refused to vote for John A. Macdonald at the request of Mr. Smith. The assistant warden testified that in the 1844 election a dozen keepers were sent by the warden to vote for his son Henry Smith Jr. in the riding of Frontenac.

Macdonald, since graced with the title "Founding Father of Canada," lived in those days only a half-mile from the prison in an oriental-style villa called Bellevue, which offered a splendid view of the lake. He so strongly believed that Warden Smith was unjustly treated by the Brown Commission that, in 1849, he tried (and failed) to set up a committee of the legislature to inquire into the conduct of the commission. Macdonald bided his time. By 1856 the political balance in the legislature was in his favour and he himself was Attorney General of the United Province of Canada. He accused the Brown Commission of recording false evidence, altering the evidence of others, suborning convicts to give false testimony, and arranging pardons for murderers in return for their false testimony. An inquiry by a committee of the legislature cleared George Brown and the commission of Macdonald's charges.[8]

The first chaplain of the penitentiary was the Loyalist William Herchmer of the Church of England. His successor, Chaplain R.V.

Rogers of St. James (Anglican) Church in Kingston, complained before the commission that the silent system was a failure. He testified that "the men talk and laugh in groups together through the yard, constantly; they know everything going on outside, and the want of discipline is quite notorious ..." The commission concluded that "the Convicts have had easy and continual opportunities of making evil communications to one another."

Tools were frequently stolen and traded for tobacco, the most common item of contraband. Plug tobacco was brought into the prison by teamsters, contractors, and boatmen. "... this tobacco was obtained by stealth and in their efforts to procure it, the Convicts served an apprenticeship in all the arts of petty thieving and deceit."

Testimony against Frank Smith, the kitchen steward, alleged that he shot arrows at convicts and caused the loss of sight in one of convict John Abraham's eyes, threw potatoes at convicts, referred to Catholic convicts as "damned papist buggers," forced convicts to open their mouths to see if tobacco was hidden, and sometimes spit into their mouths or threw salt inside, raced around the yard with the fire engine for the purpose of drenching prisoners after which he punished them to meals of bread and water for needing dry clothes, kicked a Black convict brutally, shook the Box containing a convict, and sometimes poured water on the convict in the Box.

OTHER FAILINGS REVEALED IN THE REPORT

The stableman White was "horridly" drunk one evening. He was flogged with the cats. Convict Daly, found drunk, refused to say where he got the liquor. Daly told the warden that Mrs. Smith, the warden's wife, gave him brandy.

Chaplain Rogers brought in anti-Catholic books and pamphlets. Two convicts were flogged for having such titles as "No Peace with Rome" and "Modern Popery Unmasked."

Some convicts were overfed, while many were hungry as a result of Frank Smith's favoritism. Hungry ones were seen eating from the pig troughs. One keeper testified that he regularly let his convicts eat from the pig pen in order to get more work from them. Complaints of hunger were more numerous in the summer when the meat was more likely to be bad. Sour, mouldy, and worm-infested bread was often served.

The women's quarters, in the north wing on the second floor, were reportedly overrun with bugs and vermin.

The Brown report and the subsequent replacement of Henry Smith by D.A. MacDonell (warden, 1849–1869) resulted in a more settled period in the history of the prison. MacDonell gained the appointment partly because he was a Reformer in politics like George Brown and, indeed, like the government of United Canada in 1849. But the stench of patronage was much sweetened by MacDonell's exemplary record as an officer in the War of 1812 and the Rebellion of 1837 and as a public servant in the Eastern District of Upper Canada. A thrice defeated Reform candidate in Stormont County, MacDonell nicely fitted into the announced intention of the commission to place the prison under a humane administration such that it might fulfill its proper destiny — the reform and rehabilitation of the convict.

Chapter Three
Stability and, Yes, a Touch of Humanity

With ready-made opinions one cannot judge a crime. Its philosophy is a little more complicated than people think. It is acknowledged that neither convict prisons, nor the hulks, nor any system of hard labour ever cured a criminal.
— Fyodor Dostoyevsky, *The House of the Dead.*

Warden MacDonell steered the penitentiary purposefully along economic lines. He was under instructions from the two-man board of inspectors to make the place self-sufficient. This was to be achieved by letting out to outside contractors the labour of convicts and the extensive shop space of the prison. The pattern was already set by his unworthy predecessor; in 1849, when MacDonell took over, there were five manufacturers operating inside the walls: E.P. Ross for shoes; J. and W.S. Stevenson of Napanee for cabinet-making; a certain Brown for tailoring; a Stevenson who did blacksmithing for the firm of J.P. Millner of Kingston; and S.T. Drennan, also for cabinet-making. Products made by the prison contractors were sold at retail shops in Kingston and were on display at the nearby Crystal Palace.[9]

The cabinet-maker Samuel Drennan gained a contract in early 1860 to refurbish Alwington House on King Street in anticipation of the visit of the young Prince of Wales, who would ultimately become King Edward VII after succeeding his mother, Queen Victoria. Drennan outfitted the house with the finest mahogany, walnut, and rosewood pieces, all for naught, as it turned out. The Prince never came ashore at Kingston because of a dispute over welcoming arrangements between the Orange Order and the Catholic population. Some of the furniture is now at the Donald Gordon Conference Centre in Kingston. An armchair of elaborate design with the royal arms carved into the top of its frame sits in Memorial Hall at Kingston City Hall.

A drawing of Warden Donald Aeneas MacDonell as lieutenant-colonel of the Glengarry Militia as published in *Volunteers and Redcoats, Rebels and Raiders* by M.B. Fryer (artist unknown).

The Warden's Report for 1858 listed 211 convicts at shoe-making, 55 at cabinet-making, 63 at blacksmithing, and 56 making agricultural implements. The contractors paid the warden one shilling and six pence per day per convict, money which went into the general revenue of the prison. In the middle 1860s, after the changeover to the dollar system, Drennan was paying 35 cents per convict per day; Thompson, Knox and Company paid 40 cents for each of a hundred convicts to make malleable iron for five years. Some of the best homes in Kingston were adorned with furniture made inside the walls. Earlier opposition from the Mechanics Institute to this outrageous perversion of the market system had abated by 1858. Towards the end of the century, labour unions would take up the cudgels of opposition again, and successfully.

The Protestant chaplain Hannibal Mulkins, as well as the Catholic chaplain Father Angus MacDonell, were opposed to contract labour for moral reasons. Mulkins wrote in his 1856 report[10] as follows:

> It [contract labour] promotes intercourse among the convicts, by bringing them from all the wings of the prison; it associates the oldest and the youngest together; the worst and the least culpable; the inexperienced boy and the hardened villain; and by allowing them to speak concerning their work, affords an opportunity and pretext to converse on other things; it gives the servants of the contractors an opportunity to communicate whatever they please to the convict, and to carry on a clandestine correspondence for them.... Is it not possible that the convicts could be instructed in trades under some system that would rather tend to exalt their minds than to deprave them?... the employment of the men by contractors interferes so far to prevent their secular instruction, that several convicts have not been able to learn even to read.... In an establishment whose avowed purpose is to reform the convicts, it would seem that every convict should be entitled, at least, to sufficient tuition, to enable him to read the word of God.

Mulkins's *cri de coeur* hints that there was a rough classification of prisoners under the new warden, the young separated from the hardened cases, the best separated from the worst. If that was the case, it was not mandated in the regulations of the day. The chaplain supported the doctrine of silent reflection leading to penitence. That did not alleviate in the least his bitter resentment against a system of labour that perpetuated illiteracy and ignorance of Christianity.

The male convicts not doing contract work — 325 in total — did stone-quarrying and cutting, prison carpentry, and oakum-picking (pulling out the short strands of hemp from pieces of worn-out rope to be used as caulking material on boat decks), prison cleaning, and housekeeping. The women convicts, under the supervision of Mrs. Walker, the matron, spent most of their time in their below-ground quarters beside the north wing doing sewing and work related to the shoe contract. A few worked in the prison hospital. In 1858, the women's section of the prison was pronounced self-sufficient.[11]

North cell block with the low-slung women's prison attached c. 1890. Courtesy Queen's Archives.

Edward Horsey was the prison architect in 1858; he was fully engaged in supervising the final stage of construction of a new shop building, snugged up to the east wall. (That building was converted to an isolation prison in 1887, a place away from the general population for the most mentally defective and the worst-behaved convicts. After several changes in use, it finally became, in the 1980s, a regional centre for the treatment of psychiatric cases.) Also, at this time, Horsey was planning the construction of the grand dome over the rotunda, which was completed in 1861.[12]

The architect, Horsey, was in frequent contact with Dr. Litchfield, the Medical Superintendent of Criminal Lunatics, and with William Coverdale, another architect of local renown. Coverdale had already left a lasting legacy at the penitentiary in his design of the east, west, and north wings and the powerfully impressive North Gate and Lodge, the latter finished in 1845.

In 1856, John A. Macdonald's Liberal-Conservative government purchased Rockwood Villa from Sarah Cartwright, widow of the late John Solomon Cartwright, together with its surrounding fields and hardwood groves on the slope west of Hatter's Bay. The land would be the site for asylum buildings drafted by Coverdale. The refurbished stone horse stable near the villa was full of female lunatics long before the new building was commenced.

> Oh, would to God that I were able
> To build a house like Cartwright's stable.
> For it fills my heart with great remorse,
> To be worse housed than Cartwright's horse.[13]

The new asylum, when completed in the early 1860s, would house many of the madmen kept in woeful condition in underground cells in the penitentiary. Warden MacDonell had for years been greatly troubled by the lunatics, whose pathetic noises under the dining hall made an embarrassing mockery of the rule of silence. The medical superintendent of the asylum later reported that 120 prisoners in the Provincial Penitentiary became insane between 1835 and 1871. By modern mental health criteria, the number would surely have been twice as large.

Work on the asylum started in 1859 with gangs of convicts supplying the labour under Coverdale's supervision. Rockwood, the name that slipped into the vocabulary of Kingstonians as a synonym for "a mad house," was designed to hold three hundred patients, a mix of criminal and noncriminal lunatics. In 1877 that unhappy mixture ended when the province of Ontario gained exclusive control of the institution. Thereafter, no space was allowed for criminal lunatics and the penitentiary across the bay, once again, had to find space for the most demented and most melancholy of convicts.

The rooms at Rockwood were spacious compared with the tiny cells at the penitentiary, but the windows were barred as in a jail. Gradually, it too became a prison of a different kind; the inmates languished in their rooms, out of touch with their families but in possession of opportunities for socializing well beyond the dreams of the prisoners at K.P.[14]

The puritanical rectitude of Warden MacDonell in the management of the prison was more than matched by his strictness in enforcing the rules of discipline. Wolfred Nelson wrote the Inspectors' Report for 1858 wherein he said that the yard was levelled, "leaving no place for skulking and hiding," and that a large tank of water for firefighting had been installed in the ground. He worried that the number of prisoners punished by meals of bread and water was "certainly large" but reassured himself that the guards had been instructed to be humane and kind without sacrificing discipline.

Nelson also commented on the female prison, saying that the matron, Mrs. Walker, had acquired a new sewing machine and that her unit was self-sufficient, thanks to the shoe contract. He complained of an overflow requiring that eight women be bedded down in the corridor, which made it very difficult to prevent "contamination ... at night." He thought the overflow should be sent to the Magdalen Asylum for wayward women in Montreal, run by the Sisters of Mercy; he added that there should be a completely separate prison for women, one that would cost less because female turnkeys would be paid less. He believed that female prisoners in a male prison had "an exciting and bad effect."

The Inspectors' Report also hinted at the need for vegetable gardens as a means of controlling scurvy in winter. Vegetable storage would be improved when the lunatics were moved from the basement of the dining hall to Rockwood. Finally, Inspector Nelson noted that revenue from contract labour totalled $44,000.00 against expenditures of $90,155.86 for the operation of the prison in that year — regrettably, a long way from a profitable operation.

The Warden's Report in 1858 was a confession between the lines that the economy of the prison was the controlling influence on almost everything that occurred inside the walls. He worried about the depression that beggared the country in the late 1850s and how this was hurting the sales of the manufacturing contractors and was possibly accounting for an increase in crime, thus forcing up the numbers of prisoners. He fussed that contractors and their managers were not enforcing the rules of the penitentiary, especially the rule of silence. He advised that "Convicts not employed at contract labour ... should be brought to the Quarry to the north of the Penitentiary enclosure to get stone for public buildings [in Kingston and elsewhere] which can be cut in the Penitentiary yard." Again, the gleam of potential profit shone brightly from the warden's eye.

The acid test of humanity in MacDonell's administration lay in the record of punishment of the prisoners. Assuming, generously, that all punishments were recorded, the 1858 report shows over seven thousand punishments to bread and water, about the same number as at the end of the Smith regime of horror. There was, however, an increase in the prison population. Flogging with the cat-o'-nine-tails was drastically reduced: from 101 times in 1846 to eight times in 1858. The Box, that devilish coffinlike device, disappeared under MacDonell. But a new punishment appeared — the Shower. Of this innovation, the warden wrote "This last system of punishment has been introduced from the United States Prisons and requires to be used with great care and to be seldom resorted to; in fact, none but convicts of robust constitution should be showered."

The warden's caution becomes clear from a description of the device.[15] The miscreant's head and arms were secured into wooden stocks so that his head, tilted forward, could be locked into an open-topped container. Above was a barrel of cold water which, on a signal, was emptied over the prisoner's head inside the container. The cold water rapidly built up around his head until it was completely submerged. Within a minute or two the water drained away around the prisoner's neck and down his body, rapidly enough that he did not drown but slowly enough that he felt sure he would. Some American experts testified to its effectiveness as a deterrent to bad behaviour!

MacDonell favoured the use of the willow switch on junior convicts. That punishment was used thirty-five times in 1858, an average of eight cuts per switching on the bare buttocks. The cats were used only eight times in the year, twenty lashes on average at a time. A few prisoners were chained at their work. "The chain," wrote the warden, "is resorted to as a punishment as well as a precaution to restrain those convicts who are a danger to the keepers and guards as well as to the convicts. Two of this class are now chained, though kept employed at stone breaking."

The Triangle, a modern reproduction. The convict, stripped to the waist, had his ankles lashed to the base of the uprights and his wrists at the top. His chest rested against the wide centrepiece. A cat-o'-nine-tails is visible. Courtesy Correctional Service of Canada Museum Collection.

The strapping bench succeeded the Triangle. It was used for whipping convicts at K.P. until the 1950s. The convict was required to move into the ankle slots to allow his legs to be immobilized. With bare buttocks showing, he bent over the table so that his upper body could be strapped onto the top of the bench. The leather paddle rests on the bench. Courtesy Correctional Service of Canada Museum Collection.

Here is a short selection of severe punishments exactly as recorded in the Punishment Book during these middle years of MacDonell's tenure[16]:

1. Thomas Cummings — for throwing his work about the bench when spoken to by the Keeper. Said dam you. Will not go before the Warden. Kicked his Keeper in the leg and attempted to get his scissors, turned around when leaving and held up his fist at his Keeper and used threatening and violent language.
    — 12 cuts of the switch.
    — chained and confined to Dark Cell until further notice.
2. John Thompson — for refusing to work when ordered by the Deputy Warden and for giving insolence.
    — This being a worthless and desperate man, it is ordered that he be confined in the Dark Cell until further orders.
3. David Emery — for throwing bread through cell window and telling guard he didn't care a dam for him and he would fix him.
    — 6 meals of B.& W., 7 cuts of the switch and Dark Cell until further notice.
4. David Emery [a fortnight later] — for laughing at breakfast and telling guard to shut up.
    — 6 meals B.& W., 6 cuts of switch.
5. Joseph Charboneau — for re-establishing sore on his thigh where he formerly produced a larger sore with some caustic substance.
    — 5 meals B.& W., 36 lashes with the Cats.

These, on the other hand, were typical mild punishments:

1. Quinlan — for noise at dinner when Warden was talking.
    — 6 meals B.& W. and 1 night without bedding.
2. Hunt — for having two hankerchiefs, a piece of newspaper and tobacco.
    — 4 meals B.& W.
3. Barnes — disorderly conduct in church.

    — 6 meals B. & W., 3 nights in Dark Cell.

4. Aldridge — for having pencil, paper, looking glass and tobacco in cell.

    — 4 meals B. & W.

5. [Group of 5 prisoners] — for laughing and talking in shoe shop.

    — 5 meals B. & W. and 1 night without bedding.

The warden ended his 1858 report on punishment with this revealing remark: "I have occasionally spoken to well-disposed convicts on their leaving the institution, in reference to the effects of punishment; in general it was their opinion that the cats could not be dispensed with, and the discipline could not be sustained without them, besides the fact that they [the cats] could be resorted to, had the effect of restraining the evil-disposed [convict]." That convoluted sentence probably says more about the state of the warden's conscience than about the true opinion of the departing prisoners.

This rather odd passage appeared in the warden's 1858 report. "I have considered it my duty ... to prevent evil-disposed persons from scaling the walls from the outside during the night-time, of the practicability of which we have had sufficient evidence.... I have therefore doubled the guard on night parole in the yard."

Some months earlier, a 17-year-old boy named Hardy, who had served a term in prison and been discharged, decided he wanted back in again. The prison was his community, his source of emotional security. By night, he climbed to the top of a pile of cordwood stacked on the outside of the west wall from which he was able to scale to the top and let himself down the inside with a rope. In the process he fell and hurt his leg, but not so seriously as to prevent him from stealing some money from the clerk's office. He was able to get to the horse stable where he stayed in hiding for many hours. Hardy was tried and sentenced to do further time in the prison. One result of the Hardy escapade was a new regulation which forbade stacking any material against the outer side of the prison wall.

Other persons reporting in 1858 were the chaplains, the surgeon and the schoolmaster. Protestant chaplain Mulkins outlined the fierce workload borne by him and his assistants. He was responsible for the moral and educational well-being of more than 450 convicts. (Everybody who was not a Catholic was deemed to be a Protestant.) Morning and evening services featuring Scripture readings and prayer; Sunday church service; schooling for the illiterate; religious conversations in the workplaces and on the ranges; and up to a thousand letters written for convicts. These exertions on behalf of convicts added up to a heavy burden of work. "It is in the night work, after the prison is closed, visiting the cells of every convict under his charge [the chaplain spoke of himself in the third person], going from cell to cell, along narrow gangways, consoling, warning, advising convicts, that the clearest insight into their real moral condition is obtained and the greatest satisfaction afforded of the good effected in this prison."

Mulkins happily reported that the Superintendent of Schools for Canada West, the redoubtable Methodist Egerton Ryerson, donated 500 books to the prison library. As a result, "After their meals, and on Thursday before service commences in the chapel, almost every prisoner may be seen with a book in his hand." Further on, the chaplain made a related point: "It may not be amiss to suggest again the utility of lighting up the wings [the ranges] in the evening with gas or otherwise so that the convicts may see to read in their cells.... During nearly six months [they] are shut in their cells at 5 p.m. but the cells are so dark they cannot see to read. For hours they remain there a prey to bitter reflections. Were the wings lighted, it would afford them a few hours of useful reading each day, and convert a period now looked upon as the most terrible in their imprisonment into a means of enjoyment and mental and moral cultivation." The chaplain went so far as to recommend gas lighting in the yard at night as a way to minimize escape attempts.

By 1870, artificial light was permitted into certain cells as a reward for good conduct.

Mulkins again attacked the system of contract labour, but from a different angle. He noted that convicts in the shoe shop, for example, did the same simple procedure over and over again. "He never makes a whole shoe or boot.... When he leaves he can neither cut out a boot nor make it when cut out for him. To this there are occasional exceptions, but, like angels' visits, few and far between."

The chaplain was more than justified in suggesting an end to morning and evening religious services on the ranges. "No man can go into the ranges at that time and remain there for prayers without receiving into his lungs this foul air, charged more or less with particles of matter exhaled from the lungs of 300 convicts during the night.... Some [convicts] may be putting away their beds, others sweeping their cells; some may be talking, laughing, coughing or making other offensive noises; others may be washing themselves or at their night buckets; and should all these things happen at once, during prayers, it is impossible for the guards on duty either to prevent it or to detect the offenders." Mulkins proposed, instead, a daily service in the chapel after the noonday meal.

Father Angus MacDonell, the Catholic chaplain, in his brief report expressed satisfaction with the small number of French Canadian convicts in relation to the population of French and Catholic Canada. He was pleased with the behaviour of his charges at religious services but added, sadly, "A certain few, however, seem perfectly callous to every religious feeling ... as if they had extinguished every spark of religion and every virtuous sentiment in their souls, and live apparently without remorse ... or any distant preparation for eternity."

Dr. James Sampson, the surgeon, reported an outbreak of scurvy which led to the death of a few prisoners. He wrote, "The difficulty of procuring healthy potatoes in sufficient quantity this season is as great as that of last year; but I understand the Warden has laid in a liberal supply of esculents, such as cabbages, carrots, onions, etc. — the first of which when preserved in the form of what is commonly called 'sour-krout' is considered one of the best anti-scorbutic articles of food." He recommended putting the penitentiary acres north of the walls under tillage, thereby employing many convicts, particularly the older ones, while making the institution self-sufficient in vegetables.

The schoolteacher James T. Gardiner, under the purview of the chaplains, wrote for the 1858 report much about the progress of the child convicts under his care. Most of them, he pointed out, were recently removed and sent to the new reformatory for boys at Isle Aux-Noix. That, in turn, gave the teacher more time for adult prisoners who "have been brought up and lived, until sent here, in the utmost depths of ignorance."

The teacher spent much time instructing prisoners at night while standing at the gates of their cells. He stated that he was doing cell-gate instruction for fifty prisoners in English, three in German, two in Italian, and one in Spanish. He called for the acquisition of a thousand more volumes for the library. "That reading is the most powerful preventative of the irksome ennui consequent upon seclusion, no one can doubt for a minute; indeed if we had no other means of judging than the eagerness by which the convicts seek after books, and run any risk of punishment in lending, exchanging, and bartering with each other, although strictly forbidden, we should consider that sufficient to prove the estimation in which they hold them."

This 1858 snapshot of the MacDonell regime can be suitably framed with words from departing convicts in response to "Liberation Questions." Before a released prisoner walked out the north gate clothed in a suit just removed from a new arrival, he was required to answer a set of questions put to him, usually by the chaplain. Here is a short selection from the thirty-eight liberation questions with the answers of several different convicts pulled together.[17]

> Qu. #6. During the time you were in your cell did you hear any conversation or know of any communication between the convicts?
> Macfarlane: Has heard French talked in the cells.
> Clark: Has heard them ask for tobacco.
> Roberts: Has not, but convicts will talk if they can.
> Cook: Has heard noise and whistling.

> Qu. #10. Should [if] the cells be made wider, would they contribute to the comfort of the convicts?
> Butler: Thinks not.
> Black: It is wide enough as it is.
> Crotan: They are wide enough.
> Clark: It would in taking down their bed. [The beds

were nearly as wide as the cells and were stood on end
during the daytime.]
Pringle: Thinks it would.

Qu. #16. Which, in your opinion, is the best method of
enforcing the observance of prison discipline —
punishment by Keepers as practised here or
confinement in a Dark Cell with privation of food?
Macfarlane: The Cats is better for the health of the
prisoner than the Dark Cells.
Clark: The Cats; the prison cannot be protected
without them.
Crotan: Cannot say; has never had either.
Mathews: The Dark Cell.
Roberts: The Dark Cell but was never in it.
Garceau: The Cats.

Qu. #28. Do you consider the treatment of the convicts to
be harsh or humane?
Butler: Does not think the treatment harsh.
Macfarlane: They are too well treated.
Crotan: Those who do their duty are well treated.
Alexander: Thinks it humane.
Brown: Well treated.

Qu. #35. What do you consider to be the cause that led
you into the commission of the offence for which you
were sent to the Penitentiary?
Butler: When he was taken [arrested] he was into the
liquors and cannot say whether he was guilty or not.
Macfarlane: False information.
Crotan: The liquor.
Clarke: Drunkenness.
Robert : Being out of money and no work.
Cook: Liquor.
Garceau: Bad company.

CHAPTER FOUR
AFTER SIXTY YEARS

Whilst we have prisons, it matters little which of us occupies the cells.
— George Bernard Shaw, *Maxims for Revolutionists*

Donald Aeneas MacDonell went to his well-deserved retirement in 1869 and died soon after in Brockville. Following a brief tenure by J.M. Ferres, the distinguished office of warden, Kingston Penitentiary, passed in 1871 to John Creighton, former mayor and police magistrate of Kingston. He was known for his virtues — a sound family man with a reputation for humanity and compassion. That he was a son-in-law of William Coverdale, the architect of nearly everything grand in Kingston, and a good friend of Sir John A. Macdonald greatly boosted Creighton's chances for the appointment.

Macdonald, by then well settled in as prime minister and justice minister of the newly minted Dominion of Canada, wished sincerely for his friend's success as warden. Betraying a concern that Creighton was not tough enough for the job, Sir John wrote to him advising, "There is such a thing as making a prison too comfortable and prisoners too happy." [18]

John Creighton, Warden, Kingston Penitentiary
1871–1885. Reproduction of the original is with the
permission of the City of Kingston. Correctional
Service of Canada Museum Collection.

The Creighton era, which lasted until 1885, was marked by
modest progress towards a more enlightened management. The
new federal government took ownership in 1867 of all the
penitentiaries in the Dominion. Therefore, the Provincial
Penitentiary at Portsmouth was given a new name: the Kingston
Penitentiary. The Penitentiary Act of 1868 left in its wake a new
set of regulations[19] which guided future wardens well into the
twentieth century. Some of the revised regulations signalled
change, though not necessarily progress. The cast-iron prose of
the early regulations seems tempered somewhat in the new set.

THE WARDEN
    1. The Warden shall reside in the Penitentiary as
provided by the Penitentiary Act, but shall keep his family
and servants entirely apart from the convicts.
    8. As the ... Act humanely affords to every convict the
opportunity of shortening the term of his sentence, a great
responsibility is thrown upon every officer ... to give to
every convict the exact measure of justice to which his
behaviour shall entitle him. [Therefore] ... it shall be the

duty of the Warden to be careful to select officers who are of the best moral character and who are competent for the duty, and to retain in the service those only who may prove themselves to be so.

21. He shall place under the care of the School Master every convict who requires instruction in learning, unless his conduct renders him undeserving of the privilege ...

27. When a convict is ordered for corporal punishment the Warden shall notify the Surgeon ... [and] the Surgeon shall certify in writing ... that the convict is "Fit."

29. It shall be his strict duty to see that two convicts are never allowed to occupy the same bed under any circumstances.

31. The Warden shall have the power to order night shirts to be issued to such convicts as he may consider require them, from the nature of their employment during the day.

44. The Annual Report of the Warden ... [there follows a long list of all details to be provided, including such references to individual convicts as religion, ethnicity, moral habits, education, work done, etc.]

DEPUTY WARDEN

54. He shall see that all the Officers of the Prison are supplied with Revolvers and Guards on the walls and outside the Prison with breech-loading rifles, in addition and that they are practised at stated times in the use of their arms.

62. He shall make himself acquainted with the social habits and conduct of every subordinate officer and servant ... of the Prison ... whether when he is off duty he is a frequenter of taverns or other houses of similar resort or associates with idle or loose characters, and report the same to the Warden.

65. He shall see that no material is allowed to be placed near the enclosing walls and that nothing is accessible to convicts which can facilitate escape. He shall especially see that ladders are properly secured.

66. He shall satisfy himself as to the industry, alacrity and zeal of every prisoner so that he may be able to advise

the Warden at the end of every month as to the remission of sentence.

CHAPLAIN

76. The Chaplains shall confine their religious instructions to those convicts only whose names are transmitted to them respectively by the Warden ... and they shall make no attempt to proselytize any convict.

79. They shall visit daily those convicts who are sick or under punishment and, as soon as possible, every convict just received into the prison.

84. They shall ... direct the operations of the Male and Female Schools.

SURGEON

94. Upon the reception of a convict ... the Surgeon shall inspect him for any putrid, infectious or cutaneous disease or any bodily defect and whether he has been vaccinated.

98. When a convict is ordered for corporal punishment, the Surgeon shall state in writing whether he is "Fit" for the number of lashes ordered or for any less number. He shall be present ... and shall remain while the punishment is inflicted.

106. Should any epidemic be present ... he shall make recommendations as to its extirpation or mitigation.

CHIEF KEEPER

113. He shall have charge of the dormitory cells and shall see that every one is cleaned out every morning and fresh water supplied every afternoon ... that no article marked as belonging in one cell is allowed to be placed in another.

115. He shall see that convicts are bathed regularly once a week in summer and once a fortnight in winter, unless otherwise ordered.

ACCOUNTANT

[Listed here were routine details of bookkeeping.]

STOREKEEPER

[Here we find various details of buying and keeping stores of goods.]

STEWARD

140. He shall receive all provisions of a perishable nature ... as well as forage for the horses and shall weigh or measure every article as the case may require.

145. He shall take especial care ... that the ventilation is perfect and that the utmost cleanliness prevails in the kitchen, the cellars, and in every chamber and vessel in which provisions are stored or from which they are eaten.

147. He shall see that no convict gives any portion of his mess to another.

148. He shall see that the straw in the beds is changed every three months.

150. The Steward shall superintend the shaving and hair-cutting of the convicts.

151. He shall have charge of the washing and mending of the clothing and bedding of the convicts and see that their under clothing is changed once a week and their outer clothing when necessary.

156. He shall see that every cell is furnished with one stretcher, one bed, one pillow and pillow-case, one pail, one piggin [a water bucket], one towel, one hair comb; that in summer the bed is furnished with two linen sheets, one blanket, and one rug and in winter with one blanket additional.

158. He shall see that every convict is supplied with one jacket, one waistcoat, one pair of pantaloons, two pairs of drawers, two day shirts, two night shirts when ordered by the Warden, two pairs of socks, one stock, one cap, one pair of strong shoes or brogans, one handkerchief.

SCHOOLMASTER

170. At the end of every month he shall report ... the conduct of every convict in school and his rate of proficiency to be used in determining the remission of sentence to be awarded the convict for that month.

172. The Schoolmaster shall not interfere with the religious belief of any convict except when assisting the Chaplain at Sunday School, nor hold any conversation with them on any subject whatever except by way of instruction in learning.

TRADE INSTRUCTORS
179. There shall be pains taken in instructing every convict placed under them in the trade which they are appointed to teach ... they shall be vigilant how the convict manages his work and whether he does so willingly, zealously and industriously ... They shall note whether the convict is careful to economise ... and shall take such inclination into account in making their report in the Conduct and Industry Book.

HOSPITAL KEEPER
190. As the orderlies in the Hospital will have more freedom ... it will be the duty of the Keeper to keep the stricter a watch over them. He shall be vigilant to see that the medical comforts ordered for the sick are not made use of except for that purpose and that there is no waste nor misappropriation of tea, sugar, or other articles.

194. He shall see that the bed of a patient ... is not placed within six inches distance from the wall, and if the beds are in an open ward, one bed shall never stand within four feet of another.

KEEPERS
[Their responsibilities were fewer than in 1836.]

198. It shall be the duty of the keepers to search the convicts before they leave the workshops and also the work [sites] to see that nothing improper is hid therein.

GUARDS
204. There shall be six classes of guards ... at the following salary per annum:
1. Guards Probationary (6 mos.)...........$320.
2. Guards fifth class (18 mos.)..............$350.
3. Guards fourth class (12 mos.)...........$375.

4. Guards third class (12 mos.)............$400.
5. Guards second class ....$425.
6. Guards first class ....$450.

209. The second and first classes shall be open to those guards only who have distinguished themselves for their intelligence, judgement, zeal and discretion in the execution of their duties.

212. Every guard ... must conduct himself when off duty, as well as when on duty, in such a way as to inspire sentiments of respect for his moral principles and character.

214. Every guard on the walls and on duty outside the walls shall be armed with a breech-loading rifle, in every chamber of which there shall be a ball cartridge; he shall also carry a revolver always loaded, the same as all officers within the walls.

215. He shall write daily in the Conduct and Industry Book his opinion as to the conduct and industry of every man in his gang.

THE GATEKEEPER

222. He shall permit no person apparently in liquor to enter the Prison.

[Listed also under the gatekeeper's duties were many detailed regulations regarding entry and exit at the gate.]

THE MATRON, DEPUTY MATRON AND ASS'T DEPUTY MATRON

233. The Matron shall reside in the Prison and under the general direction of the Warden and shall have the superintendence and control of the Female convicts and officers of the Female Prison.

240. She shall be careful that no means of communication can be had between the male and female convicts.

DUTIES OF OFFICERS GENERALLY

258. If any officer come to the Prison with the appearance or odour of liquor upon him; or have unauthorised communication with any convict; or be guilty of a gross neglect of duty; or of immoral conduct; of

frequenting taverns or of associating with loose characters; or of doing anything unbecoming the character of an Officer of the Institution, he shall be dismissed.

262. Every officer shall salute his superior when addressing him. All officers shall salute one another when meeting or passing when off duty.

265. No officer shall hold any conversation with another officer in the presence of a convict, except in relation to the work in hand.

277. An officer shall not make any familiarity with any convict nor permit any to be used toward him by any convict, to the slightest extent.

278. Officers shall abstain from all hasty or opprobrious language towards convicts, as entirely unbecoming their position and character.

279. No officer is permitted to strike a convict ... except in self-defense, or to suppress revolt, prevent escape, or as a punishment ordered by the Warden.

281. When a convict is obliged to retire for necessary purposes, the officer in charge shall take care that the place is so conspicuous, that the convict cannot leave it without being fully seen and that he is absent for a reasonable time only. Any delay in such cases should arouse suspicion at once and the officer must immediately make certain all is right.

288. [In using firearms to prevent an escape,] officers will bear in mind that life is to be put at hazard only under circumstances of positive necessity.

VISITORS

[There was no significant change in the rules involving visitors.]

CONVICTS

305. No convict shall give or receive any article of provisions to or from any other convict except in the presence of and with the knowledge and consent of an officer.

308. ... Convicts who are filthy in their persons, practices or habits shall also be made known to their

fellows by a distinguishing mark and shall not be permitted to eat at the same table.

315. No two or more convicts shall be together out of the sight or the easy hearing of an officer.

319. A convict is not allowed to look with curiosity nor forwardness around the room in which he is at work.

321. Every convict shall attend the services of the Church of which he has declared himself to be an adherent, nor shall he be allowed to change from one church to another without the special permission of the Directors.

328. Every convict who is seen within twenty feet of the enclosure of the prison grounds shall be liable to punishment.

RECORD BOOKS TO BE KEPT

[Regulations nos. 330 to 354 specify the record books and ledgers to be kept. Included in the long list is a Waste Book for recording the weight of the bread left by the convicts. The Conduct and Industry Book became the central guide in determining remission of sentences. The amount of remission came to be called "Good Time."]

LIBRARIES

355. There shall be a Protestant Library and a Roman Catholic Library each containing religious readings. As well, there shall be a General Library for books of general literature which shall be selected by the Library Board made up of the Warden and the two chaplains. [Governor Metcalfe who lived in Kingston, 1843–44, gave the prison a small collection of nonreligious books.]

360. No book of religious controversy nor work tending to bring into contempt either the Protestant or Roman Catholic Faiths shall be permitted to be brought into the Prison.

PUNISHMENTS

361. The punishment to be inflicted upon male convicts for any one Prison offence shall not be other than the following:

1. Diet of bread and water not exceeding nine consecutive meals.

2. Hard bed with or without a cover according to the season not exceeding six consecutive nights.

3. The two punishments above combined.

4. Ball and chain.

5. Ball and chain combined with one of the first three.

6. Confinement in the penal or separate cells with such diet as the Surgeon shall pronounce sufficient...

7. Penal or separate cell combined with one of the first three.

8. Flogging by the cats [cat-o'-nine-tails] under the restrictions set forth ... in these rules.

9. Flogging with rods of birch or other wood.

10. Shot or Weight drill.[A military punishment used for a time at K.P. The victim was required to carry a stone or piece of cement along the route of a triangle in the prison yard until he had traversed as many as twenty miles or more.]

11. Such other punishment as may be recommended by the Warden, approved by the Directors and sanctioned by the Governor in Council.

362. The punishment to be inflicted upon female convicts shall not be other than the following for any single offence:

1. Diet of bread and water not exceeding six consecutive meals.

2. Hard bed with or without covers not exceeding six consecutive nights.

3. The first two combined.

4. Cutting the hair short.

5. Ditto combined with one of the first three.

6. Penal or separate cell with such diet as the Surgeon shall pronounce sufficient...

7. Ditto combined with any of the preceding.

8. Forfeiture of days of remission of sentence....

PRISON ROUTINE

364. Summer in any rule means March 1 to October 31 and Winter means November 1 to the last day of February.

365. During summer, the prison shall be opened at 5:45 a.m. and closed at 6:30 p.m. During winter the hour for closing shall be 6:00 p.m.

367. Breakfast in summer at 6:15 a.m. and at 7:00 a.m. in winter; Dinner at 12:15 noon and Supper in the cells after closing.

369. The bell for going to bed shall be rung at 9:30 p.m. in Summer and 9:00 p.m. in Winter. When the bell is rung, convicts shall undress and hang their clothes upon the pegs.

370. The lamps allowed for good conduct convicts to read, shall be extinguished on the ringing of the last bell.

PENITENTIARY DIET

BREAKFAST Males: 1 pint pea coffee with half oz. brown sugar, half lb. brown bread and half lb. white bread or half lb. potato, quarter lb. beef, mutton or pork (with beets and vinegar twice a week).

Females: 1 pint of tea with half oz. brown sugar, half pound each of white and brown bread.

DINNER Males: One and half pint soup, half lb. brown bread, half lb. white bread or 3 qtrs. lb. potato, half lb. beef, mutton or pork.

Females: One pint soup, qtr. lb. brown bread and qtr. lb. white bread or half lb. potato, three-eighths lb. beef, mutton or pork.

SUPPER Males: 10 oz. white or brown bread, 1 pt. coffee sweetened OR 1 pt. of mush [corn meal porridge] with half gill of molasses.

Females: 6 oz. white bread, 1 pt. of tea sweetened OR 1 pt. of mush with half gill of molasses plus vegetables in season.

The reader will have noted how Victorian morality constituted the warp and the woof of the regulations of 1868. Just as school teachers at the time were forbidden to enter taverns and other places of a "loose" character, so were prison staff. Sexual mores absolutely excluded homosexual relations; indeed, specific homosexual activities such as buggery were liable to prosecution under the criminal code. No wonder then that the regulations prohibited two prisoners occupying the same bed. Neither were two prisoners ever to be allowed together in a privy nor even beyond the sight of the guard.

Also emerging from the powerfully coercive prose of the regulations is a sense of calm confidence in the superiority of the staff. The definition of the means for controlling convicts rings with certitude; one can hardly imagine anything going awry. The very length and comprehensiveness of the document reveal the benefits of experience and the serene confidence of know-how learned over past years. In the process, the viability of the institution had, by 1868, become more important than the welfare of the inmate.

Those in charge of public service institutions, whether jail or hospital or school or nursing home, often refer to this state of affairs, by which the be-all and the end-all is institutional viability, as "professionalization"; and they enjoy describing themselves as "professionals." That this process bears little resemblance to the high moral and academic standards of the three historical professions — divinity, medicine, and law — has never troubled this raft of modern "professionals." The highest compliment one can pay a good worker is to call him or her a "pro."

The elaborate trivia of institutional management contained in the nearly four hundred regulations neither directly nor indirectly address the possibility of convict reform and the building up of character. In that respect, the leadership (the chief inspector of penitentiaries and the minister of justice) still placed undue reliance on the benign effect of a stern staff, hard work, rigid discipline, and silent reflection.

A distinct advance in penal theory is evident in the principle of days of remission of the sentence as a reward for good behaviour. However, the application of the principle, as we shall see, soon fell into a well-established pattern of arbitrariness, repression, and manipulation.

CHAPTER FIVE
A KINDER, GENTLER JAIL — FOR A WHILE

The vilest deeds like poison-weeds
Bloom well in prison-air:
It is only what is good in Man
That wastes and withers there:
Pale Anguish keeps the heavy gate
And the Warder is Despair.
  — Oscar Wilde, *The Ballad of Reading Gaol*

Soon after Creighton settled his family into the impressive Warden's House at the top of the limestone shelf overlooking the north gate, he instituted a softer style of administration. (It has been said that John Creighton accepted the post on the rock-hard condition that he and his family would not live inside the walls regardless of what the regulations said.)

The principle of reducing a portion of the sentence for good behaviour became, for a while, the keystone of discipline within the prison. Days of sentence remission received the happy tag "Good Time." The flip side of that coin was the near-abandonment of the more barbaric forms of corporal punishment. Though strapping, lashing, and the ball and chain remained in the catalogue of possibilities until well past the middle of the twentieth century, their use steadily diminished while such totally demonic devices as the Shower and the Box disappeared entirely.

Indeed, until Creighton's time, there were only sticks and no carrots to control the prisoners. As we have seen, discipline during the first thirty-five years was almost exclusively a physical matter: the discipline of work, the discipline of the sleeping cell, the discipline of the inspection corridor, the discipline of physical punishment. Those who disobeyed the rules felt the bodily effects of the cats or the Dark Cell or food deprivation. Of course, this is not to say that the prisoners, both men and women, did not endure mental agonies and anxieties from their unnatural confinement: in the official record, 120 became insane during those early years. Rather, it is to say that the prison staff never gave a thought to serving the mental and emotional needs of their charges. Recall that the regulations specifically forbade any "familiarity" between guard and prisoner.

The new principle of psychological management as a more advanced means of reforming and rebuilding the prisoner resulted in the use of privileges and punishments, about evenly balanced. John Creighton was personally suited to such a judicious blend; he was fair-minded to a fault, believed in the inherent goodness of the human being, and did not have much faith in physical punishment. A few notations from the punishment book during the late years of Creighton's tenure (he died in 1885) demonstrate the point.[20] In the excerpts that follow, the guard's report, in the guard's own words, is followed by the warden's punishment decision, also in his own words. Recognition of the importance of motivation (carrots and sticks) accounts for a new column in the old book *Days of Remission Forfeited* (i.e., loss of Good Time).

Oct 28, 1882 Guard L.B. Spencer - I regret to be obligedto report ... James Bramfield for striking and knocking me down without any cause or provocation while in the shop where he works. The Foreman turned to me to speak about another man. As he was about to go away, Bramfield made some insulting remarks. I said you should not do that, it will only get you into trouble. He replied, it is none of your "God dam business" and struck me twice knocking me down and started to kick me but was prevented from doing so by Convicts Demarteau and Brown.... Bramfield has always been a very bad man ... and I do not consider him a safe man to be in the Shops. I desire to express my sincere thanks to Demarteau and Brown for their timely assistance and would ask you to remember it when an opportunity offers to do something to reward them.

Warden Creighton - Convict James Bramfield admits the charge of having assaulted Mr. Spencer and he is sentenced to three dozen lashes with the Cats — to lose all remission to date and to be separately confined till further orders. Dark Cell 4 days.

It is hard to imagine that convict Bramfield would have been so boldly aggressive in earlier days. This incident raises the question whether the Creighton regime was too soft, as Sir John A. Macdonald feared it might be.

> 1883. Convict Wilson - for telling the Keeper he did not care a god dam where the stone went that he was throwing into the crib-work.
> —- Dark Cell 4 hours, Lose Light 1 month, 10 days Remission Time (RT) lost. [One of the privileges granted to convicts in the late 1860s was a lamp for reading at night. It soon became another incentive to good behaviour.]

> 1883. Convict Allen - for refusing to work, inciting others not to work and saying the dinner was not fit for hogs.
> —- Dark Cell 24 hours.

> 1883. Winslow and Brown - for having whiskey and drinking the same in the [?] room.
> —- Dark Cell 50 hours and 24 hours. 10 days RT lost.

> 1883. Convict Cardinal - for stricking [sic] convict J. Hawson with a shovel at casting time in the foundry.
> —- Judgement suspended.

1883. Convict Brown - for smocking [*sic*] in the kitchen. This is not the first time doing so.
—- Dark Cell 48 hours.

1883. Convict Hubbs - for refusing to put up 80 moulds for a day's work. Hubbs says he will put up 70 moulds and do them good but says he cannot put up 80.
—- I have inquired and believe that Hubbs can put up 80 good moulds in 4 hours. He refuses to try.
—- Dark Cell 3 days.

1883. Convict [?] - for leaving his work and holding conversation with other convicts. I told him to go to his work when he advanced towards me in a threatening manner — putting his fist in my face, saying, "Clear away from me or I'll ———. He also insulted me in other ways.
—- Turned out on the stone pile. 10 days RT lost. ["Turned out on the stone pile" meant being sent to break rock from a pile of limestone slabs kept in the yard for that purpose.]

1883. Convict Malcomson - for leaving his place and sitting around with other men talking, when checked he insisted on talking to me in a very impertinent and disorderly manner.
—- Dark Cell 48 hours.

1883. Convict Geroux - for having a skeleton key at his bench in the shop.
—- Dark Cell 3 days. 10 days RT lost.

1883. Convict Doherty - for throwing a [?] at Convict Walker and stricking [*sic*] him on the foot.
—- Doherty is idiotic and Walker admitted that he provoked him. No punishment.

1883. Convicts Jacobs and Hutcheson - for kicking Potter in the face [Jacobs]. Leaving his place and interfering in the fight [Hutcheson].

—- Dark Cell 48 hours each. 10 days RT lost each.

1883. Convict McDonald - for giving abusive language to guard in the execution of his duties and calling him names not fit to be reported by anyone.
—- Dark Cell 48 hours.

1883. Convicts Cote and Laurant - for shaking dice and refusing guard for [trying to stop them from] shaking dice.
—- Dark Cell 48 hours and 70 hours. 10 days RT lost each.

1883. Convict Laurant - for calling the guard a god-dam mean man for reporting him [see above] and using threatening language swearing by his God he would fix me if I would report him anymore.
—- Dark Cell 4 days. 10 days RT lost.

Though the overall legacy of a warden cannot be fairly estimated by a few excerpts from the punishment record, there is clear evidence that while Creighton was in charge, a degree of rebelliousness suffused the air of K.P. The silence rule was in tatters, because everyone from the warden down had forgotten its underlying theory of reform. It was a delusion in the first place that silence could be enforced amidst the hubbub of prison industry carried on in large shops and quarries. Why the rule remained in place so long after its obsolescence is one of the many perplexities in the history of the penitentiary.

The stress of the job is well captured in this paragraph in the Warden's Report of 1882, which appears on page 32 in R.E. Neufeld's M.A. thesis (Queen's) of 1993: "To govern 700 to 800 convicts and some 70 officers, such as usually make up the population of this Penitentiary, is a source of increasing anxiety — irksome beyond description; and no matter how faithfully the duty is performed the Warden receives little favourable consideration — rather detraction and fault finding, both inside and outside the Penitentiary. He has to bear the obloquy for everything which goes wrong, although the parties who censure and criticise, within the walls at least, are often the wrong-doers themselves — think they are clever if they can put the Warden in a corner."[21]

A touch of real-life vaudeville can be found in some items in Creighton's journal.[22] One day in October 1880, Creighton confided to paper:

> Gave orders to open Prison today and continued on duty till 10 o'clock when I went in the City to pass thru' Customs some [?] rubber treads for the New Asylum stairs. I returned at half past eleven by the Street Car. On alighting from the Car at the North East Tower, I noticed one of the Prison Railroad Horses coming down the road without a driver. This at once aroused my suspicion and I passed up the road, stopped the horse and enquired of the officers in charge of the Quarry gangs if the driver of the horse, Convict John McAlister, was in any of their gangs. As I learned he was not, I came to the conclusion he had run away. I detached such Officers as could be spared from the Gangs and started them in various directions to search for him. But I learned on making enquiries from Guard Priestley that McAlister had passed up the road with the Cars at half past ten o'clock and had therefore been away at least one hour — and as his uniform clothing was found near the mouth of the railroad tunnel where it enters the quarry — it was evident that he had obtained civilian clothing and that the [?] pursuit was useless. I have learned since that a convict who was discharged three days ago and who was a friend of McAlister had been seen hanging about the locality this morning. He probably assisted McAlister's escape. Of course, with so many Convicts working outside, we run considerable risk and as this is the first Convict who has got away from us in three years, I cannot complain very much. Yet if Guard [?] who was on the North East Tower from ten to twelve had exercised as much zeal as I think he ought to have done, McAlister should not have been away more than 15 minutes, instead of an hour out of his sight. His suspicions should have been aroused quite as readily as mine when he knew McAlister was out of sight

much longer than normal — and when he saw the horse some time before I did, return without his driver and when previous to this the coloured man Daniel Paul, who breaks [*sic*] on the Cars had enquired of Priestley from inside the Wall why the horse and McAlister were not down yet. McAlister was sent from the County of Kent for ten years for horse and cattle stealing. I retired after closing the Prison at 6 o'clock.

Creighton's unhappy account of the McAlister escape offers clues to several features of K.P. in 1882. Quarrying limestone for building construction in and away from Kingston was the means of hard labour for hundreds of prisoners and would continue to be so for another fifty years. When Creighton made his rueful journal entry, there was a set of iron tracks from the quarry north of the jail, south along the Palace Road (now the lower portion of Sir John A. Macdonald Boulevard), across King Street, thence along the east and south walls of the prison to the west gate facing Hatter's Bay. The tracks carried on through the west gate into the prison yard near the shop wings. A horse could haul several cars of stone at one time but had to have someone on board to apply the brakes on the downslopes — hence the black man Daniel Paul.

An old photo of a quarry scene at the Kingston Penitentiary. Courtesy Correctional Service of Canada Museum Collection

A journal entry by Creighton on April 4, 1882, has about it a whiff of managerial uncertainty.

Gave orders to open the Prison this morning. Visited the City for an hour on business. About twenty minutes past one o'clock Convict N.D. Smith employed under Guard Hurst in the Machine shop came to my office bareheaded, covered with dirt and greatly excited. He stated that soon after he went to the shop from Dinner, Convict Cotman called him from the Machine shop to examine some tools in the Blacksmith Shop. [He said] That he did not go. That Convicts Wm. Anderson and James Jennings and some others then came into the Machine shop, seized him, forced him into the Blacksmith shop and attempted to force him into a barrel of dirty water standing near one of the Forges. That by his determined resistance he prevented them from doing so. That Guard Hurst who was present and witnessed the proceedings did not interfere to protect him. After hearing Smith's statement I proceeded to the Blacksmith shop. On my way through the yard I saw the Deputy Warden and called to him. I said there was trouble in the Blacksmith shop. He said yes he believed so, that he had taken a piece of iron from Smith who was passing with it to my Office. I requested him to accompany me to the shop. He did so. On entering, I called Hurst to the door and in the Deputy's presence, requested him to explain to me what had occurred and give me the names of those convicts who were conspicuous in the outrage. He hesitated, prevaricated and partially pretended that he did not know and could not give me names. He said that half the men in the shop were implicated. That he was so frightened that he did not know what to do. That he ran for Keeper Davidson — this statement he afterwards withdrew and said he sent for him. It was quite evident to me that Hurst desired to screen the guilty parties and that he had previous knowledge of what was about to happen. Although he was present in the midst of the men and must have spotted the guilty parties — unless he closed his eyes to their disorderly proceedings — yet he would not name one of them. I sent Wm. Anderson, James Jennings and Alfred Delaire to Dark Cells. The two former admitted their guilt. Delaire denied any active interference and after further enquiry and failing to obtain corroborative testimony of his guilt, I ordered him released. If Guard Hurst had not a guilty knowledge of the affair, he showed great lack of courage and a proper sense of duty, and I propose removing him from the shop to a post outside, and placing Guard Hewton in charge who is a practicable blacksmith. Hurst remained on duty till after close of Prison.

A letter written by Warden Creighton on May 8, 1882, illustrates the centrality of the limestone industry at the prison.[23] It was addressed to H.B. Rathbun, the wealthy Deseronto lumber mill operator. At the time, Rathbun was building a church especially for his daughter's wedding. "The order for balance of cut stone for your Church will be completed on Wednesday next, so if you will send the 'Armenia' any time after that day, the stone will be ready on the dock. I laid aside our own work to finish yours, hence you are getting it sooner than expected. We will have most if not all of the remainder of the coursing stone ready this week. Yours truly etc." At the same time, Creighton was supplying stone and convict labour for the Catholic church under construction in Portsmouth Village. It is aptly called The Church of the Good Thief.

As the country slowly became industrialized under the stimulus of Macdonald's tariff policy, the contract manufacturers within the penitentiary steadily lost ground. Local businessmen resented the unfair competition of the contractors; their opposition was reinforced by the leadership of the emerging trade unions. The prison shops were to confine themselves to manufacturing exclusively for government use, including, of course, clothing and footwear for the prisoners. The last of the private manufacturers moved outside the walls of K.P. in 1886, never to return.

On July 8, 1881, John Creighton wrote to J. White, purchaser for the Northwest Mounted Police in Ottawa, as follows: "Please send me twenty five gross of common N.W.M. Police Buttons, same as last to finish up Serge Tunics and Tan Duck Pants. I am

Sir, Your obedient Servant etc." It would take a large number of tunics and pants to require 3,600 buttons — even in pre-zipper days! And it would take the women prisoners many weeks to sew them all in place.

Three wardens before and after the turn of the century: Dr. Michael Lavell (Warden 1885–1896); James H. Metcalfe (Warden 1896–1899); and Dr. John Milton Platt (Warden 1899–1912). Correctional Service of Canada Museum Collection.

Creighton's successor, Dr. Michael Lavell, wrote (using his newfangled typewriter!) on January 19, 1892, to L. Vancoughnet, Superintendent of Indian Affairs in Ottawa: "I ... submit herewith a list of prices at which I will furnish the Clothing required for Indians under Treaties 4, 7, &6.... Might I request if the contract be given to us, that there be as little delay as possible, as much of the material required has to be imported...." An attached page listed the items of clothing and their cost. Here are a few items from the list: Chief's Pea Jackets, blue, guilt [sic!] crown buttons, with gold braid one inch wide around collar and cuffs, $11.00; Chief's Trousers with red stripe one inch wide, two side pockets, $2.50; Headmen's trousers without stripes, $2.25 ; Chief's hats, black soft felt with gold braid, $1.60; Headmen's hats as above but no gold braid, $1.25; military grey flannel shirts, $1.90.

A letter from Lavell to J.G. Moylan, Inspector of Penitentiaries, Ottawa, dated February 1,1892, reveals yet another market for prison products: "I enclose herewith Bill of Lading of carts and sleighs for Regina Jail which were shipped today. I also sent by mail to the Governor of the Jail a duplicate copy.... The account for these Articles I presume will be sent to you unless otherwise instructed."

The penitentiary underwent a major overhaul, long overdue; the work was started in the 1890s and finished by the outbreak of the Great War. The miserable "mail slot" sleeping cells were replaced by cells twice as large, though still too small for long hours of confinement. Wing by wing and range by range, the interior walls of the cells were broken down and replaced with more widely spaced solid brick walls; the new cells were equipped with water and electric light. Imagine the luxury of a private flush toilet, a sink, and an incandescent bulb overhead for prisoners, most of whom came from places without such amenities. Besides the bed, there was room in each cell for a small table on which to place writing paper and books. The wider cell gates made of round iron bars faced the large windows overlooking each range — this was the reverse of the old cells, which looked inward to the fearsome and loathsome inspection corridor. The ranges themselves carried steam pipes for heat along the outside walls. Each range was equipped with an isolation cell with a solid door to ensure darkness inside and some insulation against protesting noise from the unhappy inmate inside.

As the century drew to an end, the wardenship passed from Dr. Michael Lavell to J.H. Metcalfe, a former schoolmaster and politician, and then to John Milton Platt, doctor of medicine and former member of Parliament for nearby Prince Edward. A short selection of original records from those years provides a comparison with, though not a contrast to, the Creighton regime.

A typed letter from Warden Lavell dated March 16, 1892 to J.G. Moylan, Inspector of Penitentiaries at Ottawa, gives a rare insight into the means of coping with an "unmanageable" female convict:

I beg to call your attention to the case of the female prisoner, Martha Byron, alias Kate Slattery, whose conduct ever since her arrival here has been steadily growing worse till now it is beyond all bearing. For some time, the Matron, Chaplain and myself tried to reason with her and persuade her for her own sake, to mend her ways, this had no effect and I was compelled to resort to more rigorous measures.

I have now exhausted all the punishment I am allowed to inflict without in the least subduing her vile temper.

That you may be able to form some idea of her tantrums, about three weeks ago the Matron sent for me to quell a disturbance going on between her and one of the other prisoners, when I went in I found the Surgeon, who fortunately happened to be making his rounds at the time, restraining her by force from doing violence, when he let go of her arms she picked up a bottle standing near, and threw it at the Matron, cutting her forehead, fortunately not badly.

When I ordered her downstairs she refused to go all the while using the most profane and obscene language as an example of which, she said she wouldn't go if Jesus Christ himself were to ask her. I was compelled to call in two of the officers and have her taken to the Back Ward by force, I of course being present all the time, she has since been confined in this cell where she spends her time yelling, singing and cursing in the most frightful manner at the Matrons, Surgeon, and myself at all hours of the day and night, keeping the place in a constant state of disturbance, she has threatened to throw the contents of her bucket in the face of either of the Matrons who goes near her, and her fellow convicts are now so much afraid of her that they object to take her bucket to empty it in consequence of which the stench in the vicinity of her cell is unbearable.

Her diet is under the supervision of the Surgeon, who has my instruction to make it as light as possible without injury to her health.

Before instructed to the contrary, I had her confined to the Dark Cell several times but with no better effect.

I regret exceedingly being compelled to ask that I may be permitted to resort to some other measures than those provided [in the regulations] to try and bring her to submit to the rules of the place. In the case of male prisoners, the measures are sufficient and have never failed. If left to my own discretion, I would give her a ten-minute shower bath with a small hose when unmanageable and confine her to the Dark Cell where her disgusting language at least would not be heard by the other women or place her in a straight jacket.

In all my experience it has never before been my misfortune to come in contact with any human being, man or woman, so utterly depraved and reckless. Things have come to such a pass that no other course is left, unless she is to continue to set the whole place at defiance as she is at present doing. This woman was sent from Montreal under a two-year sentence for breaking windows, from what I have heard she has been back in jail in that city frequently and was a most troublesome prisoner.

I found no response to Lavell's letter nor any hint of what was done with the woman convict.

A final memento of Warden Lavell is this entry in his journal dated January 5, 1896.

Last night about 9:30 Keeper Macauley reported that Convict John Jackson undergoing punishment in the Dark

Cell had made attempt to hang himself by means of the handle of his bucket and making a cord of his handkerchief and boot lace. He managed by kicking at his cell door to call the Guard and on door being opened he fell outside. I have no doubt it was all pretense, I came down at once and satisfied myself it was all put on. It is a habit of his when undergoing punishment to play the insane dodge. He is serving his third term and is a cunning half-breed Indian. I allowed him to remain in hospital all night until arrival of the Surgeon. I saw him again this morning. He is none the worse for his escapade. The morning very cold, 16 below zero.

Some items from the punishment book kept by wardens Metcalfe and Platt testify to life as usual in the Big House.

Sept. 22, 1898. Convict ———— - Is guilty of shouting in his cell this evening when the cell lights were turned off for a few minutes. [The prisoner did not have the means of turning on or off his own light.]
—- 5 days RT lost.

Sept. 23, 1898. Convict ———— - Is guilty of shouting in his cell this morning.
—- Dungeon for three days. [The "dungeon" was a set of cells below ground under the asylum ward; they were unlit concrete boxes without bed or any facility whatsoever except a night pail. When the heavy wooden outer door was closed, there was absolutely no light in the cell.]

Nov. 9, 1898. Convict Leduc - I went to search Leduc's cell by orders of Dep. Warden and found on his person one clay pipe.
—- 3 days RT lost.

Nov. 11, 1898. Convict Dalton - Will not get up in the morning when the bell rings, he has been warned many times, he will not get up.
—- bread and water 2 days.

Same day. Convict Livington - Has more than the regulation number of pockets in his clothes. Also, when he was searched last evening two small pieces of tobacco were confiscated.
—- 3 days RT lost.

Jan. 13, 1899. Convict Hawkes - for destroying property in his cell ... and attempting to break the leg off bedstead. At the time of writing he is hammering and shouting.
—- sent to asylum. [The asylum was located in the north half of the shop annex next to the west gate. It is currently called the C7 building. As stated earlier, Rockwood Asylum would not accept criminal lunatics after 1877.]

Jan. 15, 1899. Convict ———- for leaving his cell and running along his range and passing or getting something from a man on lower range.
—- lose large cell. [The interval of transition from the sleeping cells to the more commodious cells gave the warden another carrot to use.]

Jan. 23, 1899. [a list of 21 convicts] - for having a meeting [no details given].
—- prison of isolation for one year. [The isolation prison along the east wall was originally a shop. Extremely unruly prisoners were sent there. It is now the regional treatment centre.]

April 3, 1899. Convict ———- - for breaking from the line in front of the Tea Server demanding in a loud boisterous voice "More Tea" which I refused. He made the threat that he would show me by writing to headquarters.
—- Dark Cell 4 hours. 2 days RT lost.

Dec. 18, 1899. [list of 9 convicts] - for talking in the wing on Sunday and in their cells.
—- all deprived of light in their cells for 5 nights.

April 20, 1903. for speaking disrespectfully of the Warden [Platt], saying that old bugger has feathered his nest real

good and when I checked him for it he said that was
nothing to talk about as the Warden had got himself into
a good home and $3,000. or $4,000 a year.
—- admonished. [It was well understood that the office of
Warden was a political appointment.]

August 24, 1904. [a list of 3 convicts — Burns, Truckle,
and Lasher] - Were drunk yesterday afternoon and acting
boisterously, one being completely knocked out and the
others very unsteady on their feet. Evidently Lasher was
guilty of the theft of the liquor as he had the key to
private quarters upstairs and besides was seen in the act
of pulling empty bottles and other articles from the
cupboard. Lasher had eight keys in his possession and
was wearing an undershirt which had no number or mark
of any kind. I also found in his cell a heavy pair of dumb-
bells. When looking through the Hospital this morning,
we came across a quart whiskey bottle hidden between
the water tank and the wall, also four pairs of boxing
gloves, two sets of dumb-bells, four pipes, three cigars,
and a song book in an unoccupied cell adjoining the one
occupied by Burns.
—- 20 days RT lost each.

It appears from the punishment record that Dr. Platt tried to
enforce the silence rule with more vigour than his predecessors. It
also appears that he was largely unsuccessful in that endeavour.

In review, the interval at K.P. between John Creighton's
benign stewardship and the appointment of a commission of
inquiry in 1913 was marked by instances of internal strife, petty
corruption and inconsistent management. The penitentiary was in
a state of decline and nobody knew how to turn things around.
The massive reconstruction of the cell blocks had reduced the
number of single cells from 840 to 456. To accommodate the
pressing demand for convict beds, the north wing was converted
to cells by 1910, thereby increasing the jail's capacity to more
than six hundred. So it remained until after the riot of 1971.

The convict strike of 1899 described in the Neufeld thesis[24]
exemplifies the deepening malaise of the institution. One day in
January of the final year of the nineteenth century, forty men in

the binder twine shop refused to eat the soup at dinner. Afterwards, thirty-three of that group refused to go back to work and were confined to their cells. The remainder of the binder twine gang refused to work. One of their ringleaders was sent to the dungeon. The next day, the gang on the stone pile refused to work. They too were sent to the dungeon cells. Then the masonry gang quit work and were clapped into the prison of isolation. The blacksmith gang joined the sitdown. In the outcome, twenty-two were locked in the isolation prison for a year, ten in the same place for six months, thirty-nine lost their cell lighting and library privileges, ten were confined to the dark cells on their ranges for twenty-four to forty-eight hours and ten languished in the dungeon for a stretch of time.

The early twentieth century regime of Inspector Stewart and Warden Platt was one of tightened discipline and hard-nosed rejection of all reform ideas. Roger Neufeld's thesis refers to an acid comment by Inspector Stewart that the Kingston penitentiary was never intended to be a poorhouse nor a madhouse. The Inspector must have sensed that K.P. was sliding in those directions.

CHAPTER SIX
ON THE EVE OF THE RIOTS

"I am sure the men feel when entering it [the Roman Catholic Chapel at K.P.] *that it is a place removed and different from the remainder of the prison; that it is adorned with much care and expense in order to help them in their devotions and their religious duties, and to make them forget, while there, the irksomeness of their confinement."*
— From the report of Father Vincent Neville, K.P. Chaplain, 1895.[25]

In 1913, the Conservative government of the day appointed a royal commission to look into the management of the penitentiary at Portsmouth. There were reports of staff dissension, corruption, and poor morale inside the Big House. Two Kingston men, the lawyer George M. MacDonnell and the medical doctor Frederick Etherington, along with J.P. Downey of Orillia, were the members of the commission.

Though the overall condition of the jail got a passing grade from the commissioners, they had much to say about particular inadequacies. Some of those are summarized below:

1. The stone-breaking shop located behind the prison of isolation (now the regional treatment centre) was the place

where convicts were sent to break rock as punishment or for
lack of other work. In 1913, there were over seventy
prisoners, "some of them mere boys," spending their long
days at the rock pile. "They were arranged in rows, facing
each other, and the stone to be broken was piled in a long
heap in front of them. As the raw material was reduced to the
required size, fresh supplies were wheeled in by tenders from
the yard.... The atmosphere was charged with stone dust ...
the closets, situated at one end of the building, were poorly
constructed and foul-smelling."[26]

2. The commissioners quoted briefly from a contemporary
    report by Dr. F.H. Young, Assistant Superintendent of
    Rockwood Hospital, about the wing for the insane at K.P.
    (The insane ward was located in the former shop building
    now called C7, the upper two floors of which are once
    again, as of 1999, filled with psychiatric patients assigned
    to the regional treatment centre. What goes around comes
    around!)

> The building in which the insane are at present
> housed [1913] is, in my opinion, entirely unsuited to
> the purpose for which it is used. It is defective in
> structural arrangement, lacking in nursing and
> medical facilities and devoid of means of providing
> occupation. The physical condition of the patients
> shows the effect of improper diet, insufficient exercise
> and fresh air. Each patient is locked in his cell,
> without proper sanitary conveniences from 4 p.m. to
> 7 a.m. The door of each cell is simply a grating [which
> would offer no protection against intrusive sounds],
> and there is no provision for the isolation and care of
> noisy and filthy patients. There is no provision for the
> proper classification of patients, all of whom are
> gathered together in a large day room, the acute with
> the chronic, the old and the helpless with the
> impulsive and violent, the lucid with the demented.

For outdoor exercise, the insane inmates were infrequently
taken to the narrow space between the west side of the

building and the high west wall of the prison. Two stanzas from Oscar Wilde's *The Ballad of Reading Gaol* are apropos.

> Like ape or clown, in monstrous garb
> With crooked arrows starred,
> Silently we went round and round
> The slippery asphalt yard;
> Silently we went round and round
> And no man spoke a word.
>
> Silently we went round and round,
> And through each hollow mind
> The memory of dreadful things
> Rushed like a dreadful wind,
> And Horror stalked before each man,
> And Terror crept behind.

The commissioners went on to say, "There was evidence to show that insane patients had been punished by tubbing [which] consisted of forcibly placing a convict in a bath filled with cold water, and holding him there at the discretion of the operators.... It was abundantly clear that the tubbing ... was resorted to neither for sanitary nor therapeutic reasons but as a punishment.... In practice the mentally unbalanced citizen, who commits a crime, is sent to the provincial hospital for the insane if his derangement is detected before he is sentenced — and to the insane ward at Kingston Penitentiary if his disease be not recognized until he has for a time been incarcerated."

3.   "The regulation that no newspaper shall be allowed within the walls has been adopted, we are told, to prevent convicts from getting information about ... their pals outside.... What a comfort the newspaper would be to many an unfortunate fellow in the solitude of his cell, can scarcely be comprehended. It would break the gloom of his isolation, keep him in healthful relations with the life he has forfeited, and, no doubt, strengthen his desire to restore to good standing in society." (In 1995, the authorities at K.P. cancelled twelve of fifteen copies of Kingston and Toronto daily newspapers as an economy measure, leaving only three

copies each of two newspapers assigned to the library and segregation units.)

4. In addition to the usual punishments of the day, there was a relatively new one at K.P. in 1913, one with a peculiarly Canadian ring to it — hosing. A cell was fitted out for the purpose as follows: "The front corners of the cell have been rounded out to prevent the prisoner from getting out of range of the stream. A circular opening in the bars permits of the entrance and manipulation of the nozzle. When the water was fully turned on, the stream through the three-quarter-inch nozzle struck the opposite wall almost unbroken. From what your commissioners have seen and heard they readily agree that hosing as a punishment is effective. The victim must cry out for mercy or suffer physical collapse. But as a disciplinary agency, it should be ranked with the rack and the thumbscrew, cruel and inhuman."

5. Regarding the hospital, they note: "There is nothing in the building or equipment which justifies the name hospital. Some 36 inside cells, inferior to the cells occupied by healthy prisoners, house [the patients] ... not effective ventilation, an obsolete bucket for excreta, no sanitary appliances ... two baths and water closets hopelessly out of date..."

6. Deploring the lack of entertainment of any kind at K.P., the commissioners questioned Inspector Stewart as follows:

    Q. What is the objection to entertainment?
    A. In the first place, it causes quarrelling and jealousy as to who shall be the chief men and who shall be the performers.
    Q. ... supposing you had some people in Kingston kind enough to come out and give some entertainments?
    A. I think they [the prisoners] would be more bored than they would appreciate it.

7. In 1909 the wardens and chaplains of all the penitentiaries except one urged upon the government the adoption of a

scheme for classifying prisoners. The inspectors "dismissed the proposal to classify prisons and segregate first offenders in a separate prison or reformatory on the ground of expense, and they reported that the classification of prisoners should be left to the judicial criminologists."

8. "The industrial conditions in the penitentiaries of Canada are a disgrace ... there is not a single well-equipped, well-managed, continuously busy shop in the whole circle of prisons.... There are no goods to make and if goods were made there is no place to market them.... At the Kingston Penitentiary there are from 20 to 30 employed on the farm.... More men are not at work on the farm because of the officials' fear of escape and the trouble of looking after the workers ... The success of prison management should not be measured in inverse ratio to the number of escapes. It is possible to have absolute security and a horrible prison."

9. It was urged upon the commissioners that prisoners should be paid for their work and that manufacturing things for state use should be developed until all prisoners have gainful employment.

10. The commission recommended a system of indeterminate sentences for offenders with parole and probation possibilities for all those incarcerated. They also made recommendations bearing on the unsatisfactory conditions noted above plus others such as an end to close cropping of hair; the free issue of tobacco; the adoption of plain grey or blue prison clothes instead of the red check garb then in use; an end to hosing of convicts, confining in the Dark Cell, and shackling with ball and chain.

The MacDonell report had a minor impact on practices at the old jail. The First World War diverted attention away from prison reform with the result that things were much the same at K.P. when the 1920s began. Indeed, by the late 1920s, the place was a sink hole of despair — overcrowded, tyrannically managed, and bureaucratically swamped. The warden, J.C. Ponsford, was dogmatically wedded to work, hard work, as the only means of reforming the convicts. But, as the commissioners pointed out before the war, there was not enough work of any kind, let alone meaningful, instructive work. The latter kind was nearly nonexistent.

Warden John C. Ponsford. Courtesy Correctional Service of Canada Museum Collection.

An inmate of the Ponsford era, Dr. O.C.J. Withrow, wrote a book about his time at K.P., entitled *Shackling the Transgressor*[27]; he said that he and several guards calculated the average work per day per convict at one and a half hours, taking into account that some worked long hard days in the stone quarry or at the stone pile while others did virtually nothing.

Withrow presents in scalding language the lack of diversions and alternatives to work. The so-called school he described as a lacklustre operation that operated for thirty-five minutes each weekday after the noonday dinner hour. He said that no more than 15 percent of the convict population took lessons of any kind, that the library was a dusty assortment of castoffs from schools with scarcely more than a thousand books in whole condition, even though the prison authorities boasted of fifteen thousand volumes on the shelves. During the thirty months of Withrow's imprisonment, he wrote that there were a total of three musical entertainments by visiting groups — and that was long before radio or television became the cherished opiate of the convict.

Reading Withrow's negative description of K.P. in 1927 — bad food, incompetent staff, insufficient work, abusive punishment which included frequent paddling with a wide perforated leather strap — makes it all the more regrettable that six years earlier *yet another* attempt at reform failed almost totally. The Minister of Justice appointed a special committee made up of three liberal-minded men — the labour leader P.M. Draper, and two distinguished lawyers, O.M.(for Oliver Mowat) Biggar and Wm. F. Nickle to make recommendations for major changes in the Penitentiary Act and regulations thereunder.[28]

Nickle was a Kingstonian of fine reputation and humanitarian instincts. They submitted a report in early 1921 which should have resulted in major improvements at the old penitentiary. Alas, the changes to the Act proposed by the committee died on the parliamentary order paper as a result of an election call later in the year; the reforms were not brought back to Parliament after the election. Consequently, the old regime at K.P., essentially unchanged since Confederation, lurched along under the hard hand of Warden Ponsford. In retrospect, the circumstances in the Big House in the 1920s were the sure and certain precursor of riots, more repression, and more riots, culminating in the awful bloody spasm of 1971.

Nevertheless, it is uplifting to recall some of the Nickle/Biggar/Draper observations and recommendations. For anyone educated in the classics, there is a bonus in reading their sentences full of ballooning clauses, finally coming to an explosive point at the end. Consider this sentence: "Humanitarian opinion very properly denounces the stone pile, which, bad as it undoubtedly is, is perhaps better than complete idleness for any man; it will not either kill him nor render him mentally unsound, as such idleness in confinement almost certainly will." The committee went on to recommend a statutory guarantee of productive work for prisoners. It was to be achieved by requiring the governments of Canada to have all of their necessities, as far as practicable, manufactured in the prisons.

On the matter of keeping women prisoners at K.P., there is this observation. "One of the recognized elements of imprisonment is the deprivation of the convict of opportunities for association with the opposite sex, and altogether apart from the possibility of irregularities, an arrangement is open to the gravest objection which brings this deprivation constantly to the minds of both male and female convicts by the existence within constant view of an institution devoted to the confinement of the opposite sex." Then there is another in the long history of calls for a separate prison for women.

They recommended that convicts be paid a meagre sum for their daily work. "If anything but evil," they wrote "is to follow from punishment by imprisonment for long terms, it is, in the opinion of the Committee, essential that such provision should be made as will allow the convict to earn at least something toward the support of his dependents during his confinement or of himself after his release." Not long after, prisoners began to be paid a few pennies a day for their work.

Had the committee's views been translated into public policy in 1921, it is unlikely the riots and their painful after-effects would ever have occurred. These statements are from the report:

> Beyond food and clothing the convict is without rights and the conduct prescribed for him is that of an automaton; he is prohibited from feeling, or at least from exhibiting, any human emotion.
>
> It is no part of the purpose of imprisonment that the spirit of prisoners should be broken or that they should, when they have completed their terms, as almost all of them sooner or later will, be worse citizens by reason of their punishment.... Their physical and mental ills should if possible be cured, their efficiency increased and their habits improved. Every officer having any duties in relation to the penitentiaries or the care of convicts will govern his conduct accordingly and failure to do so will be dealt with as a breach of these [proposed] regulations. [It would take another seventy years to achieve a degree of legal compliance with what was proposed and never passed into law in 1913 and 1921.]

The committee recommended a system of classifying prisoners according to their industrial interest and ability rather than according to categories such as age, criminal record, and mental and moral condition. They also devised a plan for paying prisoners so that a portion of the total value of their production would be divided among them. Not least, they offered a rudimentary set of rights for prisoners which, a little at a time, have been granted in the intervening years.

1. A convict shall have the right to be brought before the warden to complain in person of his treatment by an officer or to make any other request which he may desire to make to the warden. [Dr. Withrow (see above) wrote that prisoners could indeed present their complaints personally to Warden Ponsford but that they risked a tongue lashing and peremptory dismissal from his presence.]

2. Every convict shall instantly obey any order ... but nothing in this paragraph shall prevent such convict from complaining to the warden of his having been compelled to obey any order.

3. [They recommended that the rule of silence be ended but with conditions that would protect the good order of the prison.]

4. To receive in the presence of a guard once in every two months ... a member or members of his family... [Withrow stated that family visits a few years later were so severely constricted by bars and screens inside the north gate and so dampened by the censoring guard's interventions that he dreaded the frustrations of a visit].

5. To write at the public expense once in every month ... to some member of his family.

6. To receive all letters on personal, family or business matters.

7. To receive from the library ... one volume and one magazine weekly.

8. To exercise himself outdoors if the weather permits in such proper manner as he desires for at least fifteen minutes in every twenty-four hours.

9. To be supplied with pen and pencil, ink and paper, in reasonable quantities, both for purposes of correspondence and of study and training.

10. To receive two ounces of tobacco weekly and to receive materials for its use... at the public expense

until a system of remunerating convicts has been established and thereafter at their own expense.

11. To receive from the publisher at his own expense, such newspapers and periodicals as are not expressly prohibited by the warden.

12. To subscribe and pay for such courses as he may desire at any correspondence school approved by the warden.

Finally, the committee railed against corporal punishment, meals of bread and water, chaining to the cell gate, the ball and chain; they listed a set of punishments that could not exceed the temporary withdrawal of rights listed above. In the event of whippings ordered by a court as part of the sentence, they recommended that a select person be named to administer such punishments as a regular duty. Dr. Withrow spoke about court ordered whippings administered in Keeper's Hall during the late twenties.

As a follow-up to the dead-letter recommendations of the 1921 committee, there are these observations by the ex-inmate O.C.J. Withrow on themes of militarism, incompetence, and corruption at K.P. just before the 1932 riot.

The militarism of the system was apparent even in the outer trappings.... The guards wore khaki uniforms with a military cut.... The under officers were required to salute the warden and his deputy whenever they might appear and a fine would be imposed if this order were not scrupulously obeyed.

The pay [for security staff] was quite inadequate to the type of service which should have been rendered.... Most of the officers had no real interest in their work.... Of the constructive principles of rehabilitation or reform, they knew nothing and cared less.... As I watched the sentinel on the northeast tower one day [from Withrow's vantage point as an orderly on the third floor of the hospital], I thought what a colourless, aimless, lazy and devastating existence.

A convict hospitalised with severe symptoms of syphilis stated that the dishes from the hospital patients were washed three times a day in a bath-tub in the hospital, which tub was also used by the inmates for bath purposes.... Dishes used in the hospital are not sterilized, but are washed with hot water in the two bath tubs, and no provision is made to keep those of infected patients from entering the large white bath tub ... in the same batch with those of patients with a clean sheet.

A few of the guards supplement their meagre pay by trucking and trading for the convicts.... Money finds its way from friends [of convicts] directly into the hands of these guards... who deliver a portion of the value in goods for the inmates. If a guard is caught carrying on such traffic, he is immediately dismissed.

When I entered the prison the food was not good ... insufficient and badly cooked.... Rotten fish could be thrown between the bars [of the cells where the prisoners now ate their meals] to the cell block floor and on the days when fish was served, the stone floor would be strewn deeply with decaying debris.... The riot of 1927 accomplished something.... The meals began to improve.... The steward had to feed the men on nineteen cents per day per man.... The food supplied was merely fuel for our bodies.

The stage was set by 1930 for upheavals within the Big House in Portsmouth. The country slipped into economic depression which, among other things, boosted the crime rate and increased the convict population accordingly. New prisons had to be built to accommodate the numbers. More significantly and more ominously, many of the new arrivals were men of intelligence and leadership skills, qualities which could be quickly turned to destructive purposes.

It is unreasonable to treat a man as an animal or an automaton while he is serving his sentence, and then at the end of it appeal to him as a human being to win back his place in society.
—Winston Churchill

Coincidental with the first major riot in the jail's history in 1932, the Ponsford era of repression and autocratic rule came to an end; the stern old warden retired, satisfied that he had done his best under tough conditions.

Dennis Curtis and Andrew Graham point out in their volume, *Kingston Penitentiary: The First Hundred and Fifty Years*, that the prisoners, in planning a demonstration for October 17, 1932, were not seeking to destroy the institution, kill the warden, and run amok on the streets of Kingston. Far from it. They wanted redress of certain mundane grievances — like more recreation time, family visits, better food preparation, and cigarette papers to go with their free-issue tobacco. (It was said at the time that Warden Ponsford banned cigarette papers because a few convicts were caught using cigarette papers to record bets in a gambling game.) Like most prisoners everywhere, they were willing enough to do their time.

The superintendent of penitentiaries in 1932, the retired general, D.M. Ormond, wrote a detailed report of the riot for his boss, Minister of Justice Hugh Guthrie.[29] Ormond placed the riot in the context of a series of disturbances dating back to the beginning of the Ponsford era, taking care at the same time not to lay much blame at Ponsford's doorstep. Here are Ormond's findings:

1. In 1921, about fifty convicts in the stone shed downed their hammers and paraded briefly in the yard. Six or seven of the leaders were seized, locked up, sentenced to ten strokes of the paddle and thirty days lost remission time.

2. In 1923, seventeen inmates were punished for complaining about the food. The warden dismissed the event as the work of riff raff and agitators of the worst kind.

3. In 1924, ten convicts in the shoe shop left their work stations and lined up to see the chief keeper for some unnamed reason. They were marched to the prison of isolation and put on a diet of bread and water. Four of them who went on a hunger strike were threatened with the paddle if they persisted. After a few days, they were all back at work.

4. In 1927, a more organized minirevolt occurred. When a protester in the tailor shop was put in a punishment cell, a series of efforts were made by groups of convicts over several days to have him released. When their protests threatened to get out of hand, three ringleaders were punished with up to twenty strokes of the paddle. The tower guards were doubly armed and ordered to shoot if disorderly convicts approached the north gate. Ormond observed that the convicts learned a lot from this incident about the need for careful planning and unified action.

5. In August of 1931, an escape plot was uncovered whereby a truck would be commandeered and used to ram the north gate. Once through the inner gate, the convicts would break into the armoury within the north gate and shoot their way out to the street and

freedom. The plot was aborted by informers; the plotters were sent to the punishment cells inside the prison of isolation, one of whom was still there more than a year later.

In the light of a decade of incipient revolt at K.P., there was much official interest in the security of the prison. Ormond feared that the unrest resulting from the Depression would infest the penitentiary; "communistic" troublemakers were a matter of concern to him as they were to the government of the day. It was Ormond's opinion that the staff at K.P. had fallen into a "lethargy" ever since the 1890s. He worried about incompetent, uneducated guards, unskilled in managing people and untrained in the use of firearms. (Guards, except those in vulnerable locations, had not carried arms since 1915.)

Inspector Gilbert Smith became acting warden of the jail after Ponsford's retirement. He and his staff were nervous and uncertain as they faced the prospect of a major riot. General Ormond visited K.P. in August, 1932, soon after his appointment as superintendent. He was shocked by poor security practices; the stage was set for large-scale trouble because nobody in a position of authority was willing to address convict complaints in a serious way.

In October, 1932, the rebels got control of the shops, after which they crowded into the shop dome to press their demands on acting warden Smith. When he refused to call Ottawa with their grievances and, instead, asked for military assistance from the army base across the Cataraqui causeway, the prisoners seized hostages and barricaded themselves in the canvas shop. Shots were fired into the shop after which a committee of inmates met with Smith and received an assurance from him that their grievances would be taken to Ottawa.

With all prisoners locked in their cells, it seemed as if the riot was over. In mounting frustration, many of the locked-down prisoners began "acting up" in their cells. They had in their midst an accomplished activist, the leader of the Communist Party of Canada, Tim Buck, jailed for sedition under the infamous section 98 of the criminal code. An Ontario court had ruled earlier that the Communist Party of Canada was illegal, thereby setting the stage for the arrest of Buck and several other party members.

The army was called back on October 20 and the guards were armed with automatic rifles and side arms. On orders, the latter went down the narrow ductways between the ranges of cells and fired through the peepholes into those cells where they detected a commotion. Seven shots were fired into Tim Buck's cell but he was not hit. One prisoner was hit in the shoulder and remained unattended for twenty-four hours.

A new warden arrived on the scene on October 24, Colonel W.B. Megloughlin. Peace was restored as the new man set about responding to some of the grievances. In earlier days, the wardens enjoyed a lot of freedom to run their jails as they saw fit. That worked well when the warden was a person of good sense and decent instincts. But if he was disposed to tyrannical methods and arbitrary decisions, the result could be retrogressive at least or disastrous at most. Hence the call of reformers such as William Nickle for more central control, that is, more standardized management. Of course, the downside of greater centralization is that persons of intelligence and imagination are likely to be hamstrung by the bureaucracy.

The mindset of senior management is well illustrated by General Ormond's concluding observations in the report of his investigation of the riot. In summary fashion, he listed all the grievances of the prisoners, in no particular order of priority. Then he listed his conclusions, which had no apparent connection to the grievances! Complaints of improperly cooked food, lack of recreation time and facilities, lack of family visits, insufficient lighting in cells, poor medical service, punishments not in accordance with the rules, denial of cigarette papers, and so on, were scarcely recognized in Ormond's conclusions. It was as if they were all humbug to him. The reasons for the riot, he concluded, could be traced to inadequate supervision of inmates, incompetent officers, lack of knowledge of the rules, and the fact of two or three troublemakers among the eight-hundred-plus convicts. He did concede that denial of cigarette papers was an issue.

The riot of 1932 spurred the tiny socialist band in the House of Commons to demand a commission of inquiry. Agnes Macphail, the first woman elected to the House (1921), had, by 1932, left the Progressive Party in order to be part of J.S. Woodsworth's Co-operative Commonwealth Federation (CCF); she was one of the small contingent of socialists who won seats in the House of Commons in the 1935 election. As early as 1933, Macphail and Woodsworth clamoured for a commission that might be a vehicle for prison reform. Though Prime Minister R.B. Bennett rejected their demands for an enquiry, the new Mackenzie King government, elected in 1935, agreed. Agnes Macphail had visited the Kingston Penitentiary and, though her knowledge was skimpy at best, she knew much more about the situation than most other M.P.s.

Judge Joseph Archambault of Quebec chaired the commission of three, which included Harry Anderson, editor of the Toronto *Globe*, a longtime critic of the penal system. The commission's terms of reference called upon it to consider the entire penal system of the country; much attention was necessarily paid to K.P., the scene of recent trouble and always the Big House of the system. "Kingston Penitentiary," the report said, "has cell accommodation for 805 inmates. The average population for the past six years (since the riot) has been 857, and on November 30, 1937, there was a staff of 180. The Women's Prison [opened in 1934] has cell accommodation for 100. Its average population has been about 40 and the staff consists of 6 female officers."[30]

The Archambault report denounced the superintendent of penitentiaries, General Ormond. Ormond, a lawyer-soldier who had served in the First World War, rigorously controlled every detail of administration of the jails. He wrote new regulations himself which increased in number under his hand to 728. The proliferation of regulations spurred on the punishment of prisoners simply because there were so many more rules to be violated. Here is how the report put the matter:

> The regulations provide so many trivial offences that may be punished in a drastic manner that it is almost impossible for prisoners to avoid committing some punishable breach of the rules. It is therefore necessary for them to exercise constant vigilance and to evolve methods of avoiding punishment. They soon become expert in the practice and, on release from prison, carry with them a habit of concealment. Dealing only with those who are reformable, as opposed to incorrigible and habitual offenders, the present prison system is bound to result in a gradual demoralization of those subjected to it. They

become spiritually, as well as physically, anaemic, lazy, and shiftless, physically and mentally torpid, and generally ineffective and unreliable.

As an example, the commission described an actual case at K.P. "The warden had tried a prisoner named Price on a charge of attempting to incite trouble and had found him guilty of two other offences mentioned in the regulations but not included in the description of the offence in the charge. He was sentenced to be flogged with twenty strokes of the leather strap. The warden reported the matter fully, as he was required to do, and forwarded a copy of the evidence to the Superintendent (Ormond) for confirmation of the sentence before it was executed.... The Superintendent, in a long answer to the warden, reviewed the evidence in detail, the manner in which it had been given, and suggested the form of answers the guards should have given, pointed out that the offences for which the prisoner had been found guilty were not covered by the charge ..." but stated, "Your award of twenty strokes of the strap is approved." The superintendent added that the convict should be kept segregated indefinitely.

Such cavalier disregard of elementary principles of justice and fair procedure might still occur in a federal penitentiary. However, the existence of the Canadian Charter of Rights and Freedoms since 1982 and the statutory outflow from the Charter have rendered such violations far less likely, particularly where the senior official of the system is personally involved.

The commission recommended, among other things, that the system be run by a prison commission of three rather than by a superintendent, that there be official outside visitors to every federal prison, that prisoners be classified by scientific methods and placed in jails designed for different levels of risk and need categories, that prisoners be paid for their labour, that programs of recreation and exercise be made a feature of routine prison activities, that a parole board be set up under the prison commission to take the place of the remission service, that all penitentiary security staff be carefully screened and trained and better paid, and that prisoner welfare services such as the John Howard and Elizabeth Fry societies receive public support.

An attempt in 1938 to pass the main recommendations into law failed in the House of Commons. Before World War II broke out, the Parliament of Canada passed a compromise bill which merely set up a three-person commission to give direction to the federal penal system in the light of the Archambault recommendations. Thus, the most comprehensive reform initiative since the Brown report of 1849 fizzled out. The Archambault thrust was thwarted by bad luck in the political timetable and a degree of political spinelessness, just as the MacDonell effort of 1913 and that of Nickle/Draper in 1921 had been. After 1939, the political energy of the nation was consumed by the war effort and the subsequent restoration of a civilian economy.

Warden Richard (Dick) Allan.
Courtesy Correctional Service of
Canada Museum Collection.

By the mid-1950s, K.P. was full to overflowing — nearly a thousand prisoners were jammed into the place. It was a time of much creativity and innovation: sports, writing, publishing, and hobbycraft blossomed under the hand of the genial warden, Dick Allan. The prisoners produced a monthly magazine called *The Telescope*, a large collection of which is stored in the Correctional Service of Canada Museum (formerly the K.P. Warden's House). The March 1954 issue contains these spirited sentences[31]:

A meeting was held ... on February 25th for the purpose of electing six managers for the Prison League ball teams. With 85 men voting, the six men elected were Roy

Thompson, Shrimp Pelley, Johnny Hance, Frank Halliday, Dinty Moore and Louie Gallow.... Our umpire's school will be in full swing by the time this goes to press.... A general call has gone out for a manager for the Saints [the K.P. baseball team].... Much has been said about our entering the Saints in the City League again this year.... Our last fight card was pretty good and seemed to be appreciated, including the visitors. Promoter Bill Rainbow is putting together another show for the latter part of this month. Our orchestra, the Solitaires, put in one of its all too infrequent appearances during intermission and opened a few eyes. Now up to eight-piece strength, they came up with some real hep stuff. Our troupe is working faithfully ... for their appearance on the Red Cross show which will be heard on the airwaves on St. Patrick's Day, March 17.

The September 1956 issue of *The Telescope* presented a sprightly column written by Bobby Cox, entitled "Sharps and Flats." Here is a brief excerpt:

I am slightly reluctant about making a statement about the formation of a Music Appreciation Group here at K.P.... It is to be hoped that it will be given a fair chance. It is to be available to anyone able to meet the following stipulations: you must own a string of digits in lieu of a name, you must wear brown denim and you must not have long sideburns. [The reader will see the irony here — all K.P. inmates answered that description]. Records will be of the latest classical variety and will be played on nothing but the latest Hi-Fi equipment [presumably, another ironic twist].... Our new auditorium [now the gymnasium] will be open no later than November ... shouldn't something be done about the stage?... Why have a building second to none and spoil it by having a hole in the wall masquerading as a stage?

Despite the cultural liveliness under Dick Allan's leadership, the pressures of overcrowding and the lack of rehabilitative programs left the old jail vulnerable. In 1954, there was an epidemic of prison riots across North America and the virus infected K.P. It started with a major fire set by the inmates in the upper reaches of the main cell block, a fire which ultimately destroyed the grand dome which had graced the western skyline of Kingston for nearly a hundred years.

The Kingston Penitentiary on fire, 1954. Courtesy Queen's Archives, George Lilley Collection.

Two days later, rioting erupted in the area of the south shops where more fires were lit. Major damage was done to the shops, as well as the loss by fire of the historic horse stable. Finally, the army and armed guards restored order. Public opinion was strongly against the prisoners, with the result that there was no persuasive call for improvement of prison conditions. The inmates were put to work repairing the extensive damage to the roof of the main cell block and the damaged shops. Instead of being a watershed for change, the riot of 1954 was little more than a conversation piece among Kingstonians.

Roger Caron's sensational book about his prison experiences, *Go Boy*, contains some colourful descriptions of K.P. in the late 1950s. About the hated gong in the rotunda of the dome, Caron wrote, "To the guards who were always grouped around it, the bell took on the proportions of a cherished symbol of authority. To the cons it was an object of repugnance and outrage, an unjustifiable punishment, a brass monster that we were convinced had been designed solely to shatter our nerves with its loud and strident ringing. Its grating sound controlled all our movements: woke us up, sent us off to work, to lunch, to supper, to secure the count, dictating when we must dummy up and when we must go to bed. Its clang reverberated throughout the cavernous dome 127 times a day! Multiply that by 365 days a year and it is not hard to imagine how the damn thing could drive a man stir-crazy."[32] It was Warden Ponsford back in the 1920s who believed that he could greatly simplify the management of the prison by more frequent use of the bell in the dome. Ponsford's belief compares with school principals who rely heavily on clanging bells to keep their schools on schedule.

Little, if anything, changed in the old prison after the 1954 riot; that is obvious from reading Caron's references to daily routines of the prison. He described the atmosphere inside the walls as follows. "It was one of constant restraint, of suspicion and bitterness and secrecy. Men let down their guard only in intimate conversation with other cons. They all wore a look that puzzled me for a while. I couldn't begin to guess the unseeing, lost-in-contemplation vagueness. Later I discovered it was the defensive expression of old-timers, choosing not to see the all-too-familiar surroundings and depressing faces around them. It was a look that grew with the years. One day I realized that I was wearing it too."

Caron wrote that most of the convicts were hungry all the time because the food was so bad; the pay was nine cents a day; a man he knew was sentenced to twenty-one days of bread and water for a breach of discipline; rats, he said, were nightly visitors in some cells.

Many years later, the penitentiary service commissioned Guy Surprenant to prepare an oral history on audiotape of K.P. during the middle years of the twentieth century. Surprenant's work is stored in the National Archives in Ottawa.[33] His long and relaxed interviews with former K.P. guards E. Bigford, G. Kenehan, S. Scrutton, and H. Bell provide an intimate picture of the jail in the 1950s and '60s — overcrowding, untrained guards, military management, minimal recreation, punishment by the book. All four interviewees were nostalgic about their early days when physical work was the accepted means of reforming a prisoner. Stan Scrutton thought that strapping — eight strokes on the bare buttocks — was effective and that if that still existed in 1980 there would be fewer assaults. Incidentally, Stan Scrutton was the warden at K.P. from 1978 to 1981.

For good or ill, reform was in the air. The first commissioner of penitentiaries, Allan J. MacLeod (1960–70), spoke publicly about the need for professional staff, better training programs and their companion piece — separation of prisoners into maximum, medium, and minimum security jails.[34] As recently as 1958, all federal prisoners were confined in eight penitentiaries that were, in all their essentials, maximum security prisons. Providing lower levels of security and more vocational training would have a salutary effect on the system. In particular, MacLeod's thinking about parole, by which prisoners would be gradually and systematically prepared for return to civilian life, would have a lasting effect on the system. But very little of this effect could be found at the Kingston Penitentiary.

By far the most destructive of the riots at K.P. occurred in April 1971. The spark of ignition was much the same as before — an accumulation of grievances that went unanswered. The tinder, however, was more flammable than in the past. The younger inmates were filled with the bravado of the sixties, outraged by the war in Vietnam, yearning for the experience of hallucinatory drugs, ready to fight for personal freedom.

In the spring of 1971 there were 675 prisoners at K.P.; they correctly perceived that they were at the bottom of the bird cage in the new classification system. Over half of them, 380 in fact, had been in jail before. A total of 103 needed psychiatric treatment. Fourteen required protective custody because of the odious crimes they had committed. Only 30 of the whole population were qualified to go to a medium or minimum security institution! As Warden Jarvis put it in a letter to the regional director for Ontario, dated January 18, 1971, "This [population at K.P.] exceeds by far the number of the type of desperate inmates that we should have in a maximum security institution."[35]

Warden Arthur Jarvis. Courtesy Correctional Service of Canada Museum Collection.

The Warden also pointed out in his January letter that there was "widespread anxiety" about transfers to Millhaven, the new super-maximum security facility nearing completion on a rocky plain east of the village of Bath. Rumours swirled within the prisoner ranks about Millhaven, an electronic wonderland that would convert prisoners into robots. "I feel sure that there are many inmates who would like to see Kingston Penitentiary a shambles before the transfer is completed," the letter added ominously.

Preventive measures were not taken. Worse still, the jail was short staffed, needing a deputy warden and several more classification officers. The classification officers (COs), later called case management officers (CMOs), were almost the only staff with any kind of personal relationship with the prisoners. "It is clear from the evidence," wrote J.W. Swackhamer in his report on the riot, "that while classification officers [case management officers] were prepared to listen to inmates' requests and grievances ... they were frequently powerless to deal with the matters placed before them." As an example, mass discipline, whereby everybody paid the penalty for a fault committed by one or a few, was a source of bitter resentment. Yet the COs could do nothing on behalf of the aggrieved inmates because it was a matter of security. And security was all that really mattered at K.P. in 1971 — as in 1871.

The riot started on Wednesday evening, April 14, in the gymnasium or recreation hall, a generous facility built in the 1960s adjacent to the main cell block. Inmates of one range about to be exchanged in the gym for those from another range had a brief opportunity to seize a guard as hostage, take his keys, seize five more hostages, and release the whole population. The warden, the regional director, and key staff persons gathered in Keeper's Hall off the Dome where, by telephone, they carried on round-the-clock negotiations with a committee of inmates. In the meantime, the rebels had smashed the hated brass gong in the centre of the Dome and barricaded all the entrances to the rotunda. (Like a broken egg shell, the pieces of brass, fully a half-inch in thickness, still sit on a shelf in the penitentiary museum in Kingston).

The *Kingston Whig-Standard* of Monday, April 19, 1971, ran a story from Canadian Press based on an interview with an ex-convict sent out of the prison on parole on the second day of the riot.

The rebellion started, he [the ex-convict] said, shortly after a guard told a prisoner [in the gym] to tuck in his shirt. The prisoner refused, the guard was grabbed and then all other guards in the immediate area were grabbed.

One of the first pieces of prison property attacked, he said, was a large bell in the cell block area. It was rung four times a day — 32 chimes at each ringing — to announce meals or recreation period.

"I've seen guys crack up because of it," he said.

The prisoners smashed the bell with lead pipes, then cheered, he said.

Yielding to inmate demands, the officials put the prisoners in touch with a Kingston radio reporter, Gerry Retzer. Through him, the inmates informed the outside world that they wanted to air their grievances by peaceful means and that the hostages would be kept unharmed. They next demanded a committee of distinguished citizens to confer with the inmates. Such a committee was quickly put together; after hit-and-miss efforts, it finally comprised the noted criminal lawyer Arthur Martin; the lawyer Aubrey Golden; a lawyer in the administration of Legal Aid, William Donkin; Ron Haggart, a columnist for the *Toronto Telegram*; and Desmond Morton, professor of law at the University of Toronto and, not by accident, Roger Caron's lawyer at the time.

From Thursday until Saturday, the Citizens Committee, in whole or in part, met with the inmates and transmitted their concerns to the administration. Swackhamer's commission reported that "the inmates complained with respect to their total isolation from society, and the illogical nature of that isolation in view of the need to integrate the inmate more effectively for a return to society ... they complained of mass punishment; the mass use of segregation and dissociation...; the man-handling of prisoners by custodial officers, and the lack of meaningful or useful work."

In more specific terms, the inmates demanded immunity from charges and punishment, surveillance by the Citizens Committee of the re-occupation of the Dome by the prison authorities, and of the transfer process to Millhaven. The immunity demand was the sticking point. The solicitor general and the commissioner absolutely rejected immunity from prosecution. Politically, they could not do otherwise.

On Saturday, Desmond Morton, displaying great courage and good will, entered the Dome and observed the hostages safely confined in one of the narrow passageways between ranges of cells. The rebel inmates had appointed their own "police" to guard the hostages. Morton brought good news. Food sent in to the inmates was being fairly distributed. He thought the stand-off could be safely ended soon; alas, he was wrong. Early Sunday morning, the inmate committee lost control of the hotheads, unleashing a wild period of uncontrolled violence throughout the main cell block. The thirteen protective custody prisoners were brought into the Dome and severely abused. One inmate was killed and another died later of injuries. The physical damage was so great that the prison was rendered uninhabitable.

Wreckage inside the Dome, April 1971. Courtesy Correctional Service of Canada Museum Collection.

By dawn on Sunday, the bulk of the prisoners wanted an end to it. They escaped to the yard through the hospital wing and submitted to the penitentiary authorities and the army that now surrounded the various wings of the cell block. The hostages were freed, physically unharmed though in poor mental condition. By the end of the day, the inmates had all been bussed to other institutions in the area and the Big House lay in ruins.

After the inmates were gone, the RCMP sent in a camera crew to record the carnage on silent film.[36] As the wandering eye of the camera drifts soundlessly up and down the desolate ranges, the evidence of human degradation and desperation is overpowering. It is left to the imagination to provide the sound and fury as beds were torn apart, cell doors twisted, range walls ripped open revealing ancient lathework underneath, porcelain plumbing fixtures fractured to let loose torrents of water, piles of shattered furniture heaped into barricades at strategic points, crudely fashioned clubs and shields ready for the final clash with the hated authority. The camera's cool eye dwelt for a moment on a forlorn banner hanging from a railing inside the Dome: "You've taken our civil rights — we want our human rights."

As a result of the massive damage done to F Block (the south wing of the main cell block), the Protestant chapel on the upper floor had to be closed.[37] Before the riot, it had been a warmly attractive sanctuary where prisoners could find serenity, some diverting reading material, and the elevating effect of stained glass over the barred windows. After the riot, some of the salvaged stained glass found its way to Pittsburgh Institution, a minimum security jail on Highway 15, northeast of the city limits.

Outside, the RCMP film recorded small groups of soldiers walking or marching about the prison yard. A few of them were lolling on a grassy slope under the April sun. Out of the high windows atop the Dome, ragged banners inscribed with defiant words flapped in the breeze.

It was Wednesday before the ringleaders of the riot were moved to Millhaven. As they moved in shackles from their buses into a corridor of the new prison, they found themselves shuffling through a gauntlet of guards with riot sticks. "Substantial numbers of them were assaulted by officers standing either on the [unloading] platform or in the corridor.... The [Swackhamer] Commission offered them [the convicts] through counsel the right to cross-examine or to lead evidence with respect to these events. They chose to do neither. We are satisfied that similar assaults occurred in a similar way on Monday and Tuesday." Roger Caron, one of the convicts moved to Millhaven, vividly described the beatings by Millhaven guards in his book *Go Boy*.

Swackhamer drew this conclusion from studying the 1971 riot: "We conclude that the connection between insurrection and maximum security is not a coincidence." It could be said, in crude terms, that the classification system had merely succeeded in turning K.P. into a toilet backed up to overflowing.

After making the general point that the failure to implement the Archambault recommendations of 1938 lay back of the riot, the report set out very specific reasons for the tragedy: "the aged physical facilities, overcrowding, the shortage of professional staff, a program that had been substantially curtailed, the confinement in the institution of a number of people who did not require maximum security confinement, too much time spent in cells, a lack of adequate channels to deal with complaints and the lack of an adequate staff which resulted in the breakdown of established procedures to deal with inmate requests.... As long as there continues to exist an antagonistic relationship of mistrust and misapprehension [between custodial staff and inmates]... the twin objectives of order and rehabilitation will not be attainable."

The commission recommended a handbook of rules and standards of punishment that would be in the hands of every inmate; an end to corporal punishment, hard bed, and restricted diet; no more loss of pay nor loss of job except for failure to perform on that particular job; the right of appeal of a decision of the Inmate Disciplinary Board [the Warden's Court] to a Regional Appeal Board headed by a judge; more time for inmates outside their cells, which in turn would require better programs and more hobbies; more freedom for inmates to decorate their cells; the appointment of a recreation director who would develop a full program of recreational and physical activity; as well as the formation of a Citizens Advisory Committee of five persons well regarded in the community who would have full access to all parts of the institution.

The common view after the riot was that K.P. as a useful jail was finished. Bulldoze it to the ground, turn it into a museum, sell the land to the university — the advice was generously offered and generally ignored. After such a cataclysm, could the Kingston Penitentiary possibly have another life?

CHAPTER EIGHT
SPEND! SPEND! SPEND!

The mood and temper of the public with regard to the treatment of crime and criminals is one of the most unfailing tests of the civilization of any country.
— Winston Churchill.

More than a generation has passed since the great riot of 1971. Though the Big House skipped a few beats after the buses took the rioters and their frightened captives away, it was soon back in business in a different guise. The former prison of isolation along the east wall became the regional treatment centre (psychiatric ward). The former women's prison in the northwest corner of the yard, untouched by the riot, was made into a classification or reception centre for all federal prisoners in Ontario. As less damaged ranges in the main cell block were repaired, an increasing number of convicts needing protective custody were housed there; enough, initially, to do the cleaning and maintenance chores of the prison while those being classified moved in and out of the jail.

Classification, long ago recommended and repeatedly delayed, consists of sorting prisoners according to their security risk and their rehabilitation needs. There are three broad

categories: maximum, medium, and minimum security. The terms
are almost self-explanatory in the sense that a maximum type is
an escape risk and is considered to be a threat to the peace and
good order of society and of the jail itself; such a prisoner must
be subjected to close supervision at all times, whereas a minimum
type is the opposite. A high wall of wire or masonry is needed for
the former but, ideally, no wall at all is necessary for the
minimum security inmate. Medium security prisoners are
somewhere in between; they are kept behind walls or a high fence
and enjoy some freedom of movement. As the classification centre
for Ontario and, as well, a safe haven for those in need of
protection from other prisoners, the Kingston Penitentiary
became a multilevel jail; that is, it housed inmates in all three
security categories.

From the beginning, as we have seen, K.P. has been under
construction or reconstruction or modification or renovation.
Chisels, pickaxes, hammers, cement mixers, and drills have been
making raucous noises almost non-stop since 1833. Every
building in the entire complex has been transformed or modified
from its original form to become more effective or more up-to-
date, some of them several times. Though the racket of
construction has been almost continuous, there have been only
two full-scale renovations since the early building frenzy of
1833–1850. The first was in the 1890s when plumbing and
electricity were installed and the cells were changed from sleeping
cells into living cells. The second was in the 1990s when ranges
and cells and administration space were beautified and updated
to suit the electronic age.

It would take a monetary expert with a background in
economic history to produce an exact cost figure in current
dollars for all of this doing and redoing. A quarter of a billion
dollars might be close. Constructing the original sleeping wings,
shops, hospital and utility outbuildings, using unpaid prisoner
labour, may have cost 50 million dollars (in 1990s currency). The
major reconstruction of the 1890s soaked up another 15 million
dollars or so in current dollars. Since 1971, capital improvements
at the Kingston Penitentiary have consumed close to 100 million
dollars in current dollars.

Resurrecting the old jail after the great riot clearly implied
that K.P. is still a worthy penal institution; hence the decision to

repair it rather than abandon it. There is very little justification in modern penal theory for that decision. Indeed, the fresh and liberal ideas of the 1960s rendered the penitentiary obsolete. Commissioner MacLeod's regime brought to the fore such new concepts as inmates or offenders rather than convicts; rehabilitation rather than punishment; correctional officers instead of guards; parole replacing days of remission, a beckoning possibility for every inmate, according to the rather subjective criteria of a greatly expanded National Parole Board; and psychological testing, group therapy, and vocational programs in anticipation of release to civilian life.

The rush of new ideas for restoring criminals to useful citizenship required fundamentally different arrangements of staff and criminal than existed at K.P. The new liberalism called for constructive and positive interaction between correctional staff and prisoner in the classroom, the vocational shop, the dining and living quarters, and in the outdoor space; recreational programs to encourage co-operation and a growing understanding of good health, both mentally and physically; daily experiences with living things, both plant and animal, to teach respect for nature's ways; and, not least, opportunities for artistic expression. Above all, there must be a degree of freedom, the right to make choices, and a minimum of tension of the kind induced by oppressive prison regimes of the past.

The Kingston Penitentiary did not and does not lend itself to these new ideas. It was designed, as we have seen, for confining, isolating, punishing, and stigmatizing criminals. One hundred years ago and earlier, the jail performed its punitive and stigmatizing task with reasonable proficiency and economy. Few expected the prisoners to be treated humanely, not even Sir John A. Macdonald who wrote to Warden Creighton cautioning him not to be too nice to the prisoners.

Since 1971, K.P. has been completely renovated without serious thought to the civic rehabilitation of its inhabitants. The political decisions to spend pots of money trying to make a silk purse out of a sow's ear have been grounded in such pragmatic considerations as a rapidly rising prisoner population related to the burgeoning drug culture and a Kingston constituency heavily dependent on the prison industry. The Pen has always been the centrepiece of prison employment in the community. It symbolizes a secure career and a decent pension for thousands of families, past and present, in and around Kingston. It would take a government of stouter heart than we have seen to tear the old jail down.

In addition to pragmatic politics, another compelling reason for maintaining the Kingston Penitentiary lies in the growing need for maximum security jails. The prison building boom across Canada in the 1960s and '70s resulted in dozens of specialized institutions housing medium or minimum security inmates. From Judge Archambault's time in the 1930s to the 1980s, the number of federal jails in Canada grew from fifteen to sixty-five. From 1959 to 1977, the federal corrections budget shot from 16 million dollars to 308 million dollars. By 1997 it had ballooned to more than one billion dollars. It is a growth industry.

The harsher wind that blew out of national headquarters in the mid-seventies cinched a secure future for the Big House. The Trudeau government of the day, hardened by the FLQ crisis in Quebec, opposed mollycoddling anybody. Day passes became hard to get. Paroles dropped like a stone from 4,368 in 1970 to 2,136 in 1976. Statutory pardons, a relic of the distant past, came to an end.[38] The abolition of the death penalty in 1976 was accompanied by mandatory life sentences with no chance of parole for first- and second-degree murderers until twenty-five years or at least ten years, respectively, had been served in jail. Such sentences are *life* sentences because the offender remains under corrections supervision until he or she is dead and buried. The replacement of capital punishment with life sentences has added dramatically to prisoner numbers and the need, therefore, to construct new maximum security prisons.

It is interesting, in retrospect, that the justice minister in 1977, Mark MacGuigan, did not view the Kingston Penitentiary as part of the set of present or future maximum security institutions. When MacGuigan was chairman of the House of Commons Sub-Committee on the Penitentiary System in Canada, he conducted extensive hearings and prison interviews through 1976–77 with the aim of restoring the penitentiary system to good health. The report of the sub-committee asserted (in wearisome repetition of past reports) that "A crisis exists in the Canadian penitentiary system [that] can only be met by the immediate implementation of large-scale reform."[39] The "crisis" was located in other prisons, from Dorchester in the east to the British Columbia Penitentiary in the west. K.P. as the classification centre for Ontario was in limbo in 1977.

The first major project at K.P. after 1971 was the addition of a second-storey floor in all of the wings of the main cell block. Originally, there were five tiers of cells rising high above a stone floor at the bottom of each wing. Iron stairways led up from one tier to the next. In the renovation of the 1890s, the number of tiers was reduced from five to four. Adding a second floor in the 1970s, so that each floor had two tiers, effectively doubled the space for inmate social activity on the ranges, such as washing clothes, passing time in conversation, or making a cup of tea. In physical terms, this marked the disappearance of the last vestige of silent reflection in a tiny cell leading to remorse and moral recovery.

The solicitor general's report for 1988–89 contained a sentence of great import for the future of the Big House: "Construction of new stand-alone facilities has been minimized by emphasizing renovations, expanding existing facilities, purchasing new space through federal-provincial agreements, and limited use, on an interim basis, of double bunking."[40] That sentence pointed directly at the Kingston Penitentiary — a new life for the old jail, a maximum security institution for the twenty-first century, would you believe!

Within a year, a 62-million dollar project to modernize K.P. was launched. That figure was a cost estimate used by people involved in the project. It is much less than the total of capital expenditures at K.P. since 1990. The assistant deputy commissioner for Ontario mailed to me capital expenditure figures at roughly the midpoint in a so-called retro-fit from 1994 to mid-1998: they totalled 36 million dollars.

The contractors worked under strict security constraints lest any prisoner get a chance to seize a hostage, hide inside a construction vehicle, or steal a tool or anything else. Tens of thousands of dollars were spent on chain-link fences and locks behind which the workers and material were confined. The plumbing/electrical crews worked like moles inside the maze of ancient tunnels that criss-crossed under the prison yard. The main north-south tunnel is about seven feet wide while the branching tunnels are much smaller, some of them no wider than three feet and no higher than five feet.

The tunnels had to accommodate lines for updated heating, water, and sewer, and up to thirty electrical conduits for various power needs such as lighting, fire alarms, special emergency alarms, intercom and telephone, closed circuit television, and locking mechanisms. All the buildings were switched from steam to hydronic heating; that is, steam carried underground from the steam plant beside the Prison For Women was converted into hot water for distribution to the convection radiators throughout the institution. (Rioters on one of the ranges in 1997 had wrecked the radiators, letting loose a flood that spread right into the central dome.)

The exterior walls of all the buildings were repaired and re-pointed using limestone meticulously matched with the old stones. The penitentiary is an official heritage building, which imposed standards of material selection above the norm. The south wing of the main cell block where the great riot of 1971 wreaked the worst damage was completely gutted and reconstructed, including a new roof. High up on the gable end of the south wing there is a badge which denotes the first year of its original construction, 1833; only the exterior walls bear witness to that early time. Inside, it's a complex of bright administration offices, elevators, lounges, program teaching rooms, and the library.

An issue of *Heavy Construction News* dated August 1993 carried a story of the retro-fit project in which the redoing of the hospital received special comment. Removing lead-based paint from the walls was a difficult task. Also, the story points out that 750 holes had to be drilled through the concrete floor and into limestone rubble below for mechanical and electrical services. The contractor did not know about the rubble that was put there when the hospital was built; it was meant to prevent convicts from tunnelling their way out. One might think that sick convicts would be a low escape risk. The official view was different: because of the greater freedom they enjoyed in hospital, they were thought to be high escape risks.

The former women's prison was turned into the administrative nerve centre of K.P., complete with an elevator that operates as smooth as silk. Gracing the centre of the dome where the hated gong used to rest on top of an old heating unit, there is now a round control post with shatter-proof glass on its pointed peak for easy gazing upward. In symbolic terms, it is a minifortress built to withstand the most frenzied rampage imaginable. The post is replete with monitors and electronic controls for all the gates that lead into the dome. No longer does any guard need to carry keys or a handgun, which might enhance his potential value as a hostage.

All of the ranges were rebuilt with a total of 431 renovated cells, each for a single occupant. The existing cell walls remained as they were from the 1890s, too little space by current corrections standards. A bunk bed with a ladder for access is located above a desktop underneath. Along the back wall is newly designed stainless steel plumbing designed to use less water and to be relatively immune to inmate tampering. A television shelf is located on a level with the bunk bed.

A row of attached pre-fab cottages in the northeast corner of the yard, where the gardens used to be, replaced the trailers for private family visits. The north gate was gutted and redone with an electronic control centre for managing the steady traffic in and out of the prison. The visiting area was enlarged and made attractive for families with children.

Even before the retro-fit was finished, repairing and upgrading started all over again as a result of a series of mini-riots which occurred in 1997. In addition, $350,000 was spent fixing up the third floor of the regional treatment centre for a baker's dozen of maximum security female prisoners who could not be safely accommodated in the new regional cottage jails for women. As it turned out, Corrections Canada abandoned the plan to move the difficult women inside the walls of K.P. as a result of a legal challenge which they risked losing. In the process, the system once again gulped down a wad of money to no effect. And the Prison For Women survived one more imminent closure attempt.

Pretty colours over smooth steel and wallboard have dispelled the gloom of the penitentiary. But the electronic controls and video surveillance have effectively reduced the practical necessity of staff-inmate interaction and thereby neutralized to a large extent the stated intention — to bring more humanity into the operation of the jail.

CHAPTER NINE
DREAM! DREAM! DREAM!

First, the prison system is not dealing primarily with the dangerous few, but rather with the hapless multitude. Second, far from protecting us, it makes the dangerous few more dangerous. Finally, prison itself is a violence creating environment that makes some previously nondangerous people become dangerous.
— Ruth Morris[41]

In recent chapters I referred to the flirtation with idealism in the 1960s and how that was soon diminished by the resurgence of the hard-liners during the 1970s and '80s. That swing of the pendulum, it was argued, saved the Kingston Penitentiary from the wrecker's ball and led on, instead, to a free-wheeling capital spending spree without enough commensurate benefits.

As the 1980s wound down, there was a staff morale problem at the Big House, sufficiently serious to cause the Ontario region deputy commissioner to mount an inquiry. He appointed two employees of the Service, G.W. Day and B. Rees, to do the job. They found a lot of apprehension, even fear, within staff ranks stemming from what Day/Rees called a subculture within the security staff that sought to rule K.P. by intimidation. (The MacGuigan report of 1977 referred to a "hoodlum" element at that time within the security staff at Millhaven.) Day/Rees opened their report by saying that, judging by the answers of the majority of staff interviewed, the work environment at the penitentiary was very poor.

The inquiry claimed that a deviant minority had gained illegitimate power as a result of the constantly changing leadership and lack of consistency at the top. The warden of the day, Tom Epp, was quoted by the *Kingston Whig-Standard* of November 23, 1989, as follows: "This is not simply a management issue, it's everybody's issue. I feel very confident that, despite this study, that we're prepared to move into the future with the feeling that we can make this place work."[42] Throughout the next ten years Warden Epp's hope has been reiterated many times over by other wardens in other contexts.

Day/Rees interviewed frontline security staff, support people, and administrators. Even though inmates were the butt of much of the intimidation and harassment, they did not interview any inmates for two reasons: they did not want to worsen poor staff-inmate relations and they did not want to expose any inmates to further harassment.

Instead, Day/Rees reviewed about thirty inmate grievances relating to improper staff behaviour over the previous year. They found a match between staff accused by inmates of unacceptable conduct and those similarly accused by other staff. Nine years later, an inquest into the death of K.P. inmate Robert (Tex) Gentles (see Chapter 11) revealed that Day/Rees were prevented from naming the offending guards at the insistence of the guards' union.

The staff problem was made worse by the fact that there were two factions within the union contending for mastery of the security apparatus of the prison. This internal struggle was so intense in 1989 that the leader of one faction was accused of hiring an inmate to poison the leader of the other faction. The 1998–99 coroner's inquest into the Gentles death offered a reason why the "goon squad" atmosphere flourished at K.P. long after the Day/Rees report. The troublemakers were never identified nor did the report ever reach national headquarters. It became a dead letter.

The oral history project conducted by Guy Surprenant in 1980 put in relief the frustration of the old guard at K.P. with new-fangled correctional philosophy. Some of those interviewed spoke of the good old days when the line of authority was simple and punishment of prisoners for lippiness or breach of the rules was swift and effective.[43] It is not surprising, therefore, that the Day/Rees study pointed to the hard-liners' control of the guards' union as their vehicle for controlling the prison as a whole.

Research within corrections is disdained by some older staff because research can reveal staff deficiencies. For instance, the massive survey of federal inmates commissioned by Corrections Canada and conducted by Price Waterhouse in 1995 (hereafter called "the 1995 inmate survey") revealed that 84 percent of maximum security prisoners across Canada disagreed with the statement "I was generally satisfied with CSC's [Correctional Service of Canada] response to my grievance."[44] A staff survey done by Corrections Canada in 1996 (hereafter called "the 1996 staff survey") gained only 43 percent agreement from a sample of guards at K.P. in answer to the statement "Sometimes staff should play an advocacy for an offender."[45]

Partly as a result of such messy situations as that uncovered by Day/Rees in 1989, a new philosophy of corrections was posted by Commissioner Ole Ingstrup.[46] With much fanfare, it burst forth in 1990 as "The Mission Statement," which, ever since, has been on the lips of the leadership. Everybody in the service was — and is — expected to nail their flag to this credo:

The Correctional Service of Canada, as part of the criminal justice system, contributes to the protection of society by actively encouraging and assisting offenders to become law-abiding citizens while exercising reasonable, safe, secure and humane control.

Five values of unassailable virtue are set out. Here are the first three:

1. We respect the dignity of individuals, the rights of all members of society, and the potential for human growth and development.
2. We recognize that the offender has the potential to live as a law-abiding citizen.
3. We believe that our strength and our major resource in achieving our objectives is our staff and that human relationships are the cornerstone of our endeavour.

Later in the Mission Statement, in the course of a discussion of the practical meaning of the prose, there is this: "...we [the service] have a responsibility to deal with [inmates] fairly, bearing in mind that they retain their rights as members of society, except those that are removed by the fact of their incarceration. It is therefore essential that we make every effort to respect the spirit of the Charter of Rights and Freedoms in all our actions."

The statement makes inspiring reading but begs some questions. For example, what particular rights *are* removed when a person enters a federal jail? You will get a different answer from the line guards than from the warden. A guard of the old school might say, "My job is security, that's what I'm paid for and that's what I do." The warden might say, "We are trying to be in full compliance with the law." And what is the difference between respecting the *spirit* of the Charter and simply respecting the Charter? It could be vast in practice. One thing is certain: the security of the prison community is paramount; any and all rights can vanish in an instant in the name of security.

Section 11(d) of the Charter declares that any person charged with an offence has the right to be presumed innocent until proven guilty according to law in a fair and public hearing by an independent and impartial tribunal. Section 12 says that everyone has the right not to be subjected to any cruel treatment or punishment. The Warden's Court, now known as the Disciplinary Court, had a notorious reputation as a kangaroo court where a "Not Guilty" verdict was virtually unknown.

There is now a judicial format in keeping with civilian standards to ensure a degree of Charter protection to inmates. The court is headed by an independent chairperson, a political appointment, and is staffed with a clerk and a duty counsel.

However, the degree of independence of the chairperson of the court is open to question. For example, the minutes of a 1997 labour-management meeting at K.P. contain an offer by the management of the institution to write to the chairperson to the effect that they viewed as unacceptable the abuse of staff (presumably verbal abuse) by inmates. The law and the regulations have always called upon inmates to keep a civil tongue in their heads. A letter from management reiterating the point could only be for the purpose of shaping the attitude of the chairperson.

The lawyer on duty may offer advice to any prisoner before the court. The routine advisor to the chairperson is a K.P. correctional supervisor who comes to the court well briefed by staff; he or she heavily influences all verdicts. As well, though it rarely happens, an inmate may hire an outside lawyer to defend him.

Despite this veneer of judicial propriety, some convicts insist that they are treated as guilty regardless of the verdict of any inside court hearing. Incidentally, it must have been more than an oversight that the comprehensive 1995 inmate survey contained not one question about the quality of the disciplinary court. Cruel treatment can still occur at the Kingston Penitentiary, a claim that will be documented later.

The government of Canada passed Bill C36 in 1992, the Corrections and Conditional Release Act. It is a *magna carta* of sorts for inmates when they suspect a violation of the law relating to their confinement and release. Equally, it is officially regarded as the touchstone of good management of the system all the way from the commissioner at the top to the correctional officer on the range. (Four years later, the 1996 staff survey at K.P. found that of the guards sampled, only 17 percent could say that they regularly applied the 1992 act in their daily work. In a follow-up question, the same meagre percentage said that the training they received for carrying out the act was good.)

The act introduced a new bedrock principle, the protection of society, as the reference point for all planning and action in the administration of the system. In that respect, the CCRA is a statutory expression of the Mission Statement of 1990.

More significantly, making community safety the operational buzzword of all corrections policy, including parole, has caused case management officers (now called parole officers), national parole board members, and parole supervisors to become unduly cautious about sending prisoners back into civil society. "Errors" in the process get spectacular media coverage and, thereafter, excited reaction from opposition members of Parliament. The end result is more rejections of parole applications, more detentions past statutory release date (the two-thirds point in the sentence), more revocations of parole, more people locked up in jail, more "objective" reliance on formalities such as programs recommended and completed successfully, longer waiting lists for programs, and, not least, more cynicism and bitterness within the ranks of prisoners.

The Toronto criminal lawyer Edward Greenspan has reached the conclusion that parole as now practised in the federal system should be abolished.[47] He argues that it is so riddled with gamesmanship, political pressures, and parole violations of a merely technical nature as to be counterproductive. Fixed sentences determined by the court would end the anxiety, deception, and mock-solemn emphasis on remorse displayed in the present parole process. Abolition of the parole system would save over twenty-two million dollars a year (at time of writing).

Anthony Doob of the Centre of Criminology at the University of Toronto deplores the present parole system in the strongest terms.[48] One of Doob's key arguments is that the present system of parole is focused primarily on the risk that a prisoner may re-offend if released under supervision into the community. Doob argues, quite correctly, that the emphasis should fall on how to reintegrate the offender into civil society. He says the present policy is upside down: "The offender who most needs supervision and control in the community is given the least amount of time, or no time at all [for that purpose]." Conversely, the offender who least needs help in reintegrating is likely to get the most preparation time. That is Alice in Wonderland stuff.

The federal solicitor general at the time, Andy Scott, released a discussion paper in early 1998, "Toward a Just, Peaceful Society," which, as reported in the newspapers, stated that there were two thousand fewer parolees on the streets and two thousand more people in jail than there were in 1992! Those startling numbers speak of a parole system driven more by fear than any positive animus. Commissioner Ingstrup has recognized and attacked the problem by calling for a reduction in the number of incarcerated offenders in relation to those under supervision in the community; he expects them to be in a ratio of 1:1 by the year 2000. If achieved, there will have to be a reduction of several hundreds in the federal prison population. Whether and how the managers of the system will adjust this plan to suit the protection-of-society principle remains to be seen.

There is already one straw in the wind. Corrections Canada has announced a plan to add 236 halfway house beds to the existing stock of approximately 350 beds. But there has been no corresponding announcement of improved reintegration programs and activities commensurate with such an increase in halfway house populations. The John Howard Society of Ontario fears that the halfway houses are on their way to being prisons with another name.

Returning to the CCRA, here are selections from the act that illuminate the *magna carta* analogy.

33. Where an inmate is involuntarily confined in administrative segregation,... the institution ... shall conduct a hearing to review the inmate's case, and, conduct ... further reviews at prescribed times and in the prescribed manner, and, recommend to the institution head after each review whether or not the inmate should be released from ... segregation.

36. An inmate in administrative segregation shall be visited at least once every day by a registered health care professional.

40. An inmate commits a disciplinary offence who
    (a) disobeys a justifiable order of a staff member;
    (b) is, without authorization, in an area prohibited to inmates;
    (c) wilfully or recklessly damages or destroys property that is not the inmate's;
    (e) is in possession of stolen property;
    (f) is disrespectful or abusive toward a staff member in a manner that could undermine a staff member's authority;
    (g) is disrespectful or abusive toward any person in a manner that is likely to provoke a person to be violent;
    (h) fights with, assaults or threatens to assault another person;
    (i) is in possession of, or deals in, contraband;
    (j) without prior authorization, is in possession of, or deals in, an item that is not authorized by a Commissioner's Directive or by a written order of the institutional head [warden];
    (k) takes an intoxicant into the inmate's body;
    (l) fails or refuses to provide a urine sample when

demanded persuant to section 54 or 55 [of the CCRA];

(m) creates or participates in a disturbance or any other activity that is likely to jeopardize the security of the penitentiary;

(n) does anything for the purpose of escaping or assisting another inmate to escape;

(o) offers, gives or accepts a bribe or reward;

(p) without reasonable excuse, refuses to work or leaves work;

(q) engages in gambling;

(r) wilfully disobeys a written rule governing the conduct of inmates; or (s) attempts to do or assists another person to do anything referred to in paragraphs (a) to (r).

43. A charge of a disciplinary offence shall be dealt with in accordance with the prescribed procedure, including a hearing conducted in the prescribed manner.

44. An inmate found guilty is liable ... to one or more of the following:

(a) a warning or reprimand;

(b) a loss of privilege;

(c) an order to make restitution;

(d) a fine;

(e) performance of extra duties;

(f) in the case of a serious disciplinary offence, segregation from other inmates for a maximum of thirty days.

48. A staff member of the same sex as the inmate may conduct a routine strip search of an inmate, without individualized suspicion.

49. Where a staff member suspects on reasonable grounds that an inmate is carrying contraband or carrying evidence relating to a disciplinary offence, the staff member may conduct a frisk search of the inmate.

50. Where a staff member believes ... an inmate is carrying contraband in a body cavity, the staff member ... shall inform the [warden].

55. ... A staff member ... may demand that an offender submit to a urinalysis ... to monitor the offender's

compliance with any condition of temporary absence, work release, parole or statutory release that requires abstention from alcohol or drugs.

68. No person shall apply an instrument of restraint to an offender as punishment.

69. No person shall administer, instigate, consent to or acquiesce in any cruel, inhumane, or degrading treatment or punishment of an offender.

73. Inmates are entitled to reasonable opportunities to assemble peacefully ... subject to such reasonable limits as are prescribed for protecting the security of the penitentiary or the safety of persons.

75. An inmate is entitled to reasonable opportunities to freely and openly participate in, and express, religion or spirituality.

86. The Service shall provide every inmate with essential health care and reasonable access to non-essential mental health care that will contribute to the inmate's rehabilitation.

90. There shall be a procedure for fairly and expeditiously resolving offenders' grievances.

The clauses from the Corrections and Conditional Release Act cited above constitute a mere fraction of the whole statute. All of the sections dealing with release on parole, suspension from parole, detention beyond parole eligibility date, and other matters were omitted; this book is about the Kingston Penitentiary and life inside its walls.

The reader will have noted, particularly in clauses 68 through 90, the very substantial impact on officialdom of the Charter of Rights of 1982 and related provincial rights legislation. The rules of behaviour for inmates as set out in the act carry much baggage from the past, even the distant past, but with careful attention to rights and without the primitive notions associated with the silence rule and corporal punishment, most of which had disappeared from practice by the 1950s and '60s.

Just as the guards and keepers were fixated on illicit tobacco 150 years ago, so the new preoccupation is drugs. It has brought about an obsessive effort by the system to detect drug use, punish the offender, and eliminate the trade. At the same time, the punishment records of K.P. rarely specify illicit drugs as the driving factor in any discipline incident. Indeed, the punishment records are no longer called that; the system's appetite for euphemisms has replaced the Book of Punishments with a computerized record of "incidents."

The incident may feature assault, threatening, extortion, contraband, theft, or illicit peddling where it is commonly suspected that drugs are at the centre of it all; but the record does not say so. One or two inmates a day at K.P., totalling four hundred to five hundred a year, undergo urinalysis — the notorious "piss test." The test is conducted both randomly and, by order, on specific suspects, with about equal numbers in the two categories. The piss test, no surprise, is the subject of daily talk on every range and in every workplace in the jail. Inmates who have lost a job, been kicked out of a program, lost family visiting privileges, or been sent into segregation will frequently say that they tested positive for some substance or another or that they refused the test and paid the price in some way or another. Those caught red-handed with drugs are normally turned over to the police for prosecution outside the walls.

In 1995, a report on the drug problem generated by the Ontario regional headquarters of CSC[49] listed the following facts:

* In 1993–94, the deaths of at least nine offenders (in federal prisons) were related to drug abuse;
* Approximately 70 percent of offenders report on admission that they were either under the influence during the commission of their offences or that drugs were a major factor when committing their offences;
* Between 6 and 20 percent of the offender population report they are substantially or severely addicted to drugs and alcohol;
* Recent urinalysis statistics show that when randomly selected, at any one time, approximately 20 percent of the incarcerated population had recently taken an intoxicant. (Inmates say that the piss test has the effect of pushing them away from soft drugs like hash, which linger longer in the body to hard drugs like heroin, which flush out more quickly and are less likely, therefore, to produce a positive test result.)

The report went on to outline a strategy (another dream?) for stamping out drug use in the jails, a strategy including such measures as more urinalysis tests, closer control of contraband goods that might be traded for drugs, and more sophisticated surveillance of visitors, such as the ion scanner at the front gate, more programming related to substance abuse. The struggle to combat drug use is often at the centre of staff-inmate tension and, consequently, generates stacks of complaints and grievances by prisoners who believe their rights have been violated.

The 1996 staff survey at K.P.[50] revealed a wide difference in perception between guards and other staff on the effectiveness of the drug strategy. Eighty-six percent of the fourteen guards surveyed disagreed with the statement that the strategy had resulted in better CSC control of drugs brought in by visitors. A much smaller majority, but a majority nevertheless, of the twenty-eight other surveyed staff disagreed (54 percent). Only 27 percent of the guards agreed that urinalysis for drugs had resulted in a decrease in drug use, whereas 48 percent of the other staff agreed. The maximum security inmates across Canada in the 1995 inmate survey were closer to the guards at K.P. in their perception. A substantial majority of them (62 percent) said that the urine testing program had no effect on drug use by inmates. Only 14 percent thought that the program had resulted in a large decrease in drug use.

The *Kingston Whig-Standard* published a story on January 9, 1997, to the effect that 1,140 litres of potent brew (booze) had been found at K.P. over the previous four weeks, much of it stashed in plastic bags inside the drywall behind the heaters on the newly renovated ranges. The effect of such a warm hiding place was to produce a lot of alcoholic stuff in a short time, some of it dangerously toxic.

The life span of the Big House now approaches 175 years. Its original mission — to punish offenders and make them penitent through hard labour, enforced solitude, and stern doses of Christian teachings — all of that is now laid to rest. The past fifty years have seen new prescriptions — vocational education, schooling in literacy and numeracy, behaviour modification through psychologically based programs, privileges extended and privileges withdrawn, and "head games" employed by staff to keep the convicts uncertain, anxious, and compliant.

In recent years there has been a conspicuous lack of direction and consistency at the old jail. From 1971 to the present, there have been eleven wardens, each one with his or her own dream of success, each one bringing in new blood that was supposed to make a difference. Their dreams and plans have led to surges of purpose and bounces in morale, followed by relapse and discouragement.

The so-called C7 project, now part of the instantly forgotten history of the Big House, illustrates the malaise. An inmate's own description of the project (his identity is protected), dated May 1996, with my bracketed editorial additions, follows:

After the onset [in the early 1990s] of the massive retro-fit of the dark, dank and filthy prison known as the Kingston Penitentiary, the place was filled with tension and oppression. Cells already criminally too small for one person were now housing two. [The 45 sq. ft. cells at K.P. are about 20 sq. ft. short of the minimum standard dictated by government policy.] In an effort to alleviate some of the problems of overcrowding, C7 was opened. It comprised the two top floors of the shop building on the west side of the main shop complex. [This same space was the insane ward back in the late nineteenth and early twentieth centuries.]

Not only were the inmates screened, but any staff member wishing to work there would be as well. A selection board comprised of classification officers [case management], correctional officers II [senior guards], correctional supervisors and unit managers perused files to find 92 inmates as the most suitable ones. To give the appearance that the decision-making process would not be arbitrary, they set out guidelines. Your security classification had to be medium or minimum, you had to be following your correctional plan and you must not have been convicted within the last six months of a major crime which could jeopardise the security of C7. [The 46 rooms on each floor were twice as large as the cells in the main block. Each room housed two inmates, each one with a key to their room. All inmates had free access to the spacious hallway, laundry/showers, and common kitchenette. They also had their own dining room in the main cell block. There was a locked security gate at the end of the hall.]

Had these guidelines been adhered to, the animosity and derogatory remarks directed at C7, by both inmates and staff, would not have been as great. The rest of the population viewed C7 as PC7 (i.e., protective custody, a mini- or pseudo-prison, housing informers, special protective custody cases, management pets, etc.) and staff were viewed as wimps afraid to work in a real prison. The overall tension should have been reduced, but instead it was heightened; so they filled C7 with whomever they wanted, regardless of the criteria set out. When questioned about some of the inmates living in C7, one correctional supervisor stated, "They meet another set of criteria."

While C7 had been deemed from the beginning as a temporary arrangement [to alleviate crowding while the old ranges were being retro-fitted], it was hoped by some that if successful enough, it might become a permanent fixture. However, the axe fell much sooner than expected with a number of factors contributing to C7's demise.

Shortly before Christmas, 1995, the unit manager of C7 called a meeting where he informed the inmates that the unit would be closing and that they would be transferred to medium security institutions. Further, a number of inmates from the main cell block would be transferred as well. This was being done to allow for the expansion of space for the regional treatment centre.

Later, it was explained to the inmates by the head of RTC that the inmates were the victims of a domino effect. With the planned closing of the Prison For Women, some of those inmates requiring special attention not available in the new women's facilities could be housed at RTC. This made it all the more imperative to expand the treatment centre.

When the idea of C7 was first hatched, some said it wouldn't work within the confines of a maximum security jail. While it exceeded the expectations of many, it never lived up to its billing. Perhaps the most glaring factor in its closure was the failure to follow through on the ideology and lofty expectations voiced at its birth. Was it a ploy to attract inmates to it? When you consider all the careful planning that went into it, screening inmates and staff, the question has to be asked: Why did they place two classification officers there who were notorious for gating inmates? ["Gating" refers to detaining a prisoner past statutory release date, that is, the two-thirds point in the sentence.] Why were they not offered the opportunity to cascade down to medium or minimum security jails instead of being held back? With rising costs and budget cuts, it became increasingly difficult to justify C7 when it was little more than a human warehouse. In addition, K.P. was moving to become a true maximum security prison and C7 was viewed as an aberration. In view of these factors, C7 could be more useful as an annex to the treatment centre.

Upon learning of C7's closure, the inmates were assured that every effort would be made to transfer them to Joyceville or Warkworth or Bath [all medium security] depending on available space, programs and incompatibles. [The latter refers to other prisoners in the system who are sworn enemies of the transferee.] This seemed to be lip service in the light of the seeming pre-ordained destination of each one. When called in, each one was told, "You have been approved or pre-approved to go to a particular prison." No one was consulted nor allowed input. Any who balked were told, "Either accept this transfer voluntarily or be transferred involuntarily."

A few took this threat seriously, and rather than run the risk of being transferred to a prison they didn't want, took matters into their own hands, and using a variety of methods — failing urinalysis, threatening staff — left management no choice but to raise their security to maximum and place them back in the old cell block. Others met with their case management team and were eventually able to get to the prison they wanted.

Not surprisingly, some of these transfers were questioned by the receiving prisons. In a few cases they did not have the programs needed by the inmate to prepare him for release. Some inmates who had their security classification questioned had their cases transferred to regional headquarters for clarification.

What is of special significance is the number who moved back to the old cell block upon learning C7 was closing. When C7 first opened, inmates were told they were the cream of the crop. They were chosen as the most suitable and desirable to ensure C7 would succeed. This was the dawn of a new era in corrections. While Bath Institution had a similar set-up, it was a medium security jail. C7 was inside a maximum jail. If it succeeded, there would be more programs so that inmates could begin to cascade down through the system.

The parting words of the C7 unit manager were, "You can take pride in knowing you are responsible for C7's success, you made it work." As a reward, inmates were uprooted in a brutal and callous fashion with little or no regard for the continuity of correctional plans — all in the name of fulfilling someone's ambitions. Those who did not accept what was happening could be transferred involuntarily.

This proves once again that CSC cannot be trusted. Regardless of any program's success, if it no longer falls within the parameters of the ever-changing agendas or philosophies, or if it attempts to be successful, it will be eradicated no matter what the consequences.

For the inmates affected, this episode has been an eye-opening experience, leaving many disillusioned with the system. It did very little to inspire confidence, trust, or belief that CSC has the interests of the inmates in mind with respect to rehabilitation. The writer is of the opinion that regardless of the obstacles, actions, or treatment meted out by CSC, it should not deter an individual who is determined to change his life.

For the 92 men of C7, no longer do they enjoy the luxury of a clean, quiet, comfortable environment in a peaceful, harmonious atmosphere. It fostered positive, constructive interaction amongst themselves as well as with staff. It was a welcome break from the old cell block — "Little Beirut."

Many were transferred to other prisons where they can look forward to smaller, dirtier, double-bunked reception cells, the bottom of every program waiting list, interruption of their correctional plans, and having to prove themselves again. Of those who remain, they return to Little Beirut with their memories of C7.

To his credit, the inmate's story does not present villains and angels in stark terms. Rather, he presents, unwittingly, an example of unfolding dreams and hopes about the continuing use of the penitentiary. The inmate author of this story did not know, apparently, that C7 was never more than an expedient arrangement that would end when the retro-fit was finished. The ninety-two convicts put there in 1993 saw it differently. They looked forward to programs that would ultimately send them down the ladder to a minimum security jail. The deputy warden in 1993 hoped that the experiment in relaxed security would become a permanent fixture at K.P. But by January of 1996, the warden was saying that C7 would be transformed and made part of a prisoner mental health centre serving the province.

At the same time, the word was out that K.P. had been declared a purely maximum security institution. Those in C7 who had medium security classification either had to go to a medium security institution or be reclassified as maximum and return to the main cell block.

The C7 business happened to coincide with the need for more facilities for federal inmates in Ontario with psychiatric problems. It also coincided with a minicrisis in the housing of maximum security women prisoners across the road at the Prison For Women. In the process, ninety-two men had their lives turned upside down with a lot of consequent pain and inconvenience. There will never be any satisfactory explanation nor recompense for them.

The years 1996–97 presented an anxious public with stories about riots and lesser disturbances at Millhaven Penitentiary, twenty miles down the Loyalist Parkway near the village of Bath. The stresses emanated from the fact of an overcrowded assessment unit to which all federally sentenced convicts in

Ontario were sent for sorting and dispatch to other institutions, on the one hand, and the long-term Millhaven inmates, on the other hand, who were unhappy about many perceived deficiencies. Some of the hardened regulars at Millhaven took matters into their own hands and carried on a prolonged series of protests with much destruction of property.

After the inevitable change in administration at Millhaven and more hurried planning at the top, it was finally decided to move about one hundred of the men in the Millhaven assessment unit to newly renovated ranges at K.P. where, presumably, their assessment would be done. Bringing one hundred men or more for assessment at the old jail would necessitate sending any leftover medium security inmates still at K.P. off to some other place. It also would require different arrangements for the assessees: different gym times, different yard times, and different movement times within the Dome so that the unclassified novices would not mingle with the "max" types at K.P.

In the outcome, nobody from the assessment unit at Millhaven was actually moved to K.P. Rather, parolees in Ontario who violated one or more parole conditions were sent to K.P. instead of their home jail to await new parole hearings which would determine their fate. For a time in 1997–98, buses arrived weekly with small batches of parole revokees bearing the label TDs (Temporary Detainees). Some stayed a week and some stayed many weeks. All of them hated the stigma that goes with confinement at K.P. They were strictly segregated, without programs, and with very little employment. The TDs were not happy campers.

As stated earlier, there are several alternative uses for the Kingston Penitentiary that are worth considering. A long-term maximum security prison is the least plausible one. Maximum security prisoners need sophisticated correctional facilities designed for their therapeutic effect, not a make-over of ancient facilities suited to a penal philosophy lost in the mists of history. But having decided to make it viable and having spent huge sums of money in the doing of it, the authorities will continue dreaming about the day when all will be right at the Big House in Portsmouth.

The [Correctional] Service shall provide every inmate with (a) essential health care; and (b) reasonable access to non-essential mental health care that will contribute to the inmate's rehabilitation and successful reintegration into the community.
— Section 86, *Corrections and Conditional Release Act*, 1992

The old hospital at K.P., except for its exterior walls, is now (1998) a spanking new regional hospital with bright paint, comfortable furniture, state-of-the-art technology for dental work, adequate diagnostic facilities for minor ailments, eight beds in renovated cells, a medical doctor on site ten hours a week, and eight full-time equivalent nurses. A nurse visits the segregation ranges each day.

A little farther down the east wall is the once-upon-a-time hell hole called the prison of isolation; it is now the regional (psychiatric) treatment centre. As its title suggests, its male inmates are brought from federal institutions across Ontario. The focus of effort at the treatment centre is improving the mental health of the patients through psychological and psychiatric assessment, counselling, addiction programs, and treatment. The inmates at the centre do not fraternize with

K.P. inmates. The two populations lead completely segregated lives.

My notes about visits to K.P. since 1992 contain many references to the health concerns of inmates and how the institution responded to those needs. Here is a selection of stories derived from those notes. I make no claim to indisputable truth in these accounts; they reflect my best effort to record accurately what I had just seen and heard at the jail. The identity of the inmates is concealed with fictitious names.

SAM'S STORY

I met Sam, a Native Canadian, in early 1993 while attending a meeting of the Native Brotherhood at K.P. A big, deep-voiced man with a clean shaven head and fair complexion, he does not fit the image of a Native Canadian. But neither do many others of Native ancestry in this country.

Sam told me about his health concerns; how he was in poor physical shape and was not, he believed, receiving good treatment. At the time (1993) he said he had a bleeding ulcer, was vomiting two or three times a day, and had been able — after some effort — to have added to his prison diet milk and juice made from juice crystals; he had lost twenty pounds in weight. The head of health services at the hospital told me, when I inquired on Sam's behalf, that he should submit a request for referral to an outside specialist in internal medicine. I passed this on to Sam.

A month later, Sam told me that a doctor had earlier recommended special shoes for his troubled feet while he, Sam, was at another jail. The head of health services at K.P. told me that he should submit a request to a nurse to get information on the shoes in question. Why did that recommendation and follow-up action not follow Sam when he moved to K.P.? The best answer I can offer is that this is another instance of notoriously faulty or delayed communication where service to inmates is concerned. It is as if nobody cares.

On Friday, July 16, 1993, Sam phoned me to say that he had been in the Hole (dissociation cells) for being insolent to a guard and had, as a result, missed an appointment with the prison doctor; the guard in the Hole would not let him out to keep the appointment. Sam said that he was ill with a sore throat and was throwing up during the night. The head of health services told me that the nurse on duty whose tour included the Hole regarded Sam as a threat to her physical safety and that he would have to wait until the following Tuesday when the doctor would be back. She added that if Sam needed crisis care in the meantime, a doctor would be summoned.

In late August, Sam told me that he had been taken to the Hole for three days in mid-August and that when he was released, his special shoes plus his shorts and shirt were missing from his cell. I called the head of security who told me that he would check to see if special shoes were really needed (!) in this case.

On Friday, October 15, 1993, Sam contacted me to say that he was in hospital and throwing up blood. He said that the diet established for him the previous March had been discontinued three months ago by the kitchen steward despite the objections of the dietitian.

I had less contact with Sam during 1994 though I knew that he had been detained beyond his statutory release date and would have to do time until his full sentence was served in early 1995. Early in January of 1995, Sam asked me to enquire about the doctor's order of two months ago for special shoes for him. The nurse on duty at the hospital said she knew nothing about any order for special shoes. The prison doctor told me that he would look into the matter.

A postscript to this story: At Sam's sentence expiry date, the warden chose not to exercise his prerogative whereby he could approve special transportation funds to get him to a town in northern Ontario where he had family. The warden followed normal practice by approving sufficient fare money to get Sam to the place in southern Ontario where he had been convicted. Almost immediately, Sam got into a drunken rampage, which led to more criminal charges. He spent over a year in provincial jails, some time in a Native healing lodge, and was, for a time, in a large Canadian city trying to adjust to civilian life.

Sam's bad experiences with the health care service at the penitentiary demonstrate the negative effects of an institution where staff-inmate relations have always been in a state of undeclared war, where mutual cynicism about the motives and integrity of the other side has been endemic, and where both sides engage in defensive and self-serving language instead of open dialogue. In the 1996 staff survey at K.P., it was found that 83 percent of a staff-wide sample of fifty-three persons agreed that a good principle is not to get too "close" to offenders.[50] An inmate in poor health in such an environment has a slim chance of getting better, the more so as prisoners themselves are generally poorly informed and poorly motivated about their own health needs.

WILLY'S STORY

In the summer of 1995, I first encountered Willy — in administrative segregation at K.P. He freely admitted a serious drug problem, strongly protested the decision to move him to a maximum security jail like K.P., and beseeched me to help him get to a drug treatment centre within the correctional system. He said he was placed in segregation at K.P. because of an alleged assault against a guard in the previous medium security jail, which allegation he denied. When I learned that the assault charge against him had been dropped, a security official at K.P. told me that he was still regarded as guilty(!) and was therefore left in segregation.

In the fall of 1995, I agreed to fill a temporary vacancy on the Outside Grievance Committee, a mechanism designed to deal with certain grievances before they reach the warden's desk for final resolution. The substance of Willy's grievance was the decision of the regional treatment centre not to admit him for treatment.

The committee decided to hold off making a recommendation on Willy's grievance pending a meeting with the head of the treatment centre who, according to Willy, had told him in the course of a short encounter in segregation in the late summer that he would try to get him into the centre for treatment of his drug addiction. Accordingly, the committee felt they needed to meet with the head of the treatment centre to hear his version of what was said. On the day of the appointment, November 9, 1995, the head was not there, as we expected, and the committee was invited to meet with a male nurse who knew Willy. He told the committee that even if the head had given the inmate reason to believe that he would be admitted to the centre, he, the nurse, did not want an unsavoury, disagreeable person like Willy at the treatment centre. He also said that Willy did not meet a criterion for admission to the centre: having a major, treatable mental illness. That seemed at odds with the evidence that many inmates without major mental illness had been treated at the centre for drug addiction and related illnesses.

The committee recommended that Willy's grievance be upheld and that the treatment centre make a special exception to their admission criteria in order to put Willy under treatment in preparation for his release to a halfway house the following March. In the meantime, Willy was taken out of segregation in December, put on a range with the general population, and advised to take the regular K.P. substance abuse program. Preferring treatment at the centre, he rejected the program offered at K.P. On January 10 of the new year, the Citizens Advisory Committee asked the warden why there had been no response from his office regarding Willy's grievance. At about the same time, Willy reported to me that the treatment centre had offered him a place in their drug treatment program on condition that he sign the necessary consent form to use some of his statutory release time in order to finish the treatment centre program. That, by the way, was a 180-degree switch from the centre's position of a month earlier. The offer collapsed for reasons that are not clear. About two weeks later the warden's office rejected the advice of the Outside Grievance Committee that Willy's grievance be upheld. The warden's response was that the committee had not interviewed the head of the treatment centre. This was Catch-22 magnified, because the committee had tried to meet the head as noted above. Incidentally, the regulation time lines for responding to a grievance had, by this time, been grossly violated — nothing new.

In March, three weeks before Willy's release to a halfway house, the head of the treatment centre wrote to me explaining why their various efforts to assist Willy had failed, laying the blame on Willy for being "manipulative, mendacious, contumacious, deceitful and scurrilous." Those adjectives clanged inside my head because I had read those memorable words in a psychiatrist's report on Willy written in 1991. I responded that even a minimal application of the Mission Statement of 1990 would call for a more constructive description of an inmate and that if the same kind of commentary went out to the parole supervision people, then surely Willy's chances of success in the community were slight. I added that the principle of "protection of the public" had not been respected in this case.

Since then, Willy has failed at least twice in the community, was resentenced, sent back to K.P. to a special needs range, then transferred to a medium security jail, and, in 1999, given mandatory release back into the community.

Willy's story is the most vivid illustration in my experience of the sometimes disastrous consequences of merely punitive management of a prisoner. People like Willy — and there are many hundreds of them in jail — need keepers and caregivers who can rise above the provocative behaviour of the inmate, who can turn the other cheek and persist with kindness and constructive offers of help. That is the surest way to protect the public and the only way that is likely to work to everyone's benefit.

The very nature and tradition of the Kingston Penitentiary make one wonder whether this lesson will ever be learned by most of the rank and file who work there. According to the 1996 staff survey at K.P., 86 percent of the guards sampled thought that a military regime is the best way to run a prison. Reassuringly, strong majorities of other staff groups disagreed with the guards' outdated thinking.

BEN'S STORY

One day in the springtime of 1994, a bulky figure sitting on a retaining wall near the family visiting units at K.P. called out to me, "Are you the Citizens Advisory Committee? I want to talk to you." If I had had an inkling of what troubles lay ahead, I might have turned away and hurried on.

Ben was convicted in the mid-eighties of a horrendous crime against young foreign female hitchhikers on holiday in Canada. He was sentenced to twelve years in prison for a crime that, however serious, might have drawn six or eight years in another court.

The severe sentence meted out to Ben draws attention to the fact that many judges, if not all, assume that the offender will be paroled at or about the halfway point in the sentence. Ben was not paroled and even at the two-thirds point in the sentence, he was denied statutory release, which would have allowed him to serve the last four years under supervision in civil society. He had not taken programs that addressed his criminality and, therefore, he was considered a risk to public safety. Subsequently, he was denied parole each year for the same reason until the full twelve years were served. With each passing year the mutual hostility between prison staff and prisoner increased and, therefore, his consequent unreadiness for life outside. The thought processes of CSC staff and the parole board do not allow for this kind of logic.

Two things loomed large in the emerging picture of Ben. He was suffering from an ailment called multiple chemical sensitivity which seemed to be getting worse. The retro-fit of the old jail was at full throttle, resulting in falling chips of old paint, layers of construction dust everywhere, exhaust fumes from diesel and gasoline engines, at times ear-splitting noise, and crowded conditions on the ranges. Much of the time, though not always, Ben wore a dirty industrial safety mask to protect himself from the solids in the air. More than once, I saw him lose his coherence when he got a whiff of engine exhaust. Sometimes yellow patches appeared on his exposed skin surface. Quite frequently he walked with a limp which he attributed to allergic reactions but which may have resulted from an injured back long ago. A long list of common foods produced a bad reaction in him.

The other fact in his life, ominous in its proportions, was that he was under a deportation order to Britain the moment of his release from jail. According to a citizenship department ruling after his conviction, Ben was declared to be not a citizen. The decision was based on the fact that he was born out of wedlock of a non-Canadian woman even though his father was a Canadian. This is what happened. His father, a Canadian soldier overseas, impregnated an English girl in 1940 but failed to marry her thirty three days after Ben's birth. Legitimized by the marriage and fully documented as such, Ben was brought to Canada on a troop ship along with his mother and younger sister, all of them Canadian nationals under existing law. He spent all his life in Canada totally oblivious to the possibility that he might not be a citizen under our first citizenship law of 1947. His brief "illegitimacy" as an infant turned out to be the thin thread upon which Immigration Canada hung its decision to deport him for his crimes. Section fifteen of the Canadian Charter of Rights and Freedoms (1982) has been successfully used to confer citizenship in a comparable case (see

Benner vs. Canada 1997). That particular section of the charter bestows the equal protection and benefit of the law upon all individuals living in Canada. Given that current social morality and statute law regard children born out of wedlock as equal in rights and dignity to children born within a marriage, it is a beckoning possibility in Ben's case that he has been the victim of discrimination under section fifteen of the charter. Some crusading young lawyer will have to prove it.

A few of the security people and others at K.P. agreed that Ben had a real medical condition, but most thought he was stringing them along. An expert doctor in environmental medicine put Ben through a series of tests in 1992 and 1994 and concluded that he "suffers from environmental sensitivity disorder manifest mainly as multiple chemical sensitivity."[51] The expert recommended an isolation cell for Ben with a glass door to seal him off from the noxious effects of the jail. The cell would have special air intake from the outdoors equipped with charcoal filters. No action was taken to implement this recommendation.

Ben was offered a room in C7, more removed from the construction and with windows overlooking sunny Portsmouth harbour. He turned down the offer out of concern that he would be in the line of smoke from the Native sweat lodge that was fired up for a day from time to time. He also believed that the new materials used in renovating C7 might cause an allergic reaction.

His detention hearings each year were essentially without dialogue, partly because Ben would not enter the newly decorated room filled with synthetic materials where the hearings were held and the parole panel would not move to any other venue just to accommodate Ben. He refused again to come inside the room for the 1995 hearing and claimed to be in distress. He was taken to the Hole, where I found him resting on his bunk. The keeper in the Hole told me that the institution did not recognize Ben as having a medical problem. Despite that official view, Ben was taken to the Hole at his own request when his range floor was polished in January of 1996. Obviously, somebody agreed that he had a medical problem even though the Hole was not exactly a salubrious place for anybody, sick or well.

That same month, Ben submitted a request to prison health services for a charcoal filter mask from a supplier in the United States specializing in equipment for people with allergies — a mask that would be paid for by Ben, not the taxpayer. The request was turned down by the prison doctor and the order was cancelled. A later claim by health services at K.P. that they were trying to expedite the order for the mask was flatly denied by an official in the U.S. office with whom I talked by telephone. The Texas official told me that there was no record of any communication from any staff member at K.P. Somebody was either lying or in error.

With the help of a Kingston lawyer, Ben sued Corrections Canada for failure to care for him as the law required. The case was heard in Federal Court in Ottawa in early June 1996. Expert testimony from the specialist in environmental medicine noted above indicated that Ben could experience adverse reactions from histamine, petrochemicals, formaldehyde, tobacco smoke, and chicken. Ben's own testimony pointed to such other materials as floor wax, aftershave lotion, and incense. The doctor said in court that Ben was likely to have trouble adapting to a polluted environment while under the psychological stress of the prison and that the only known remedy was a change to an environment free of the irritants.

The K.P. witnesses for Corrections Canada were able to persuade the judge that they had earnestly tried to care for Ben, including an offer of transfer to an institution with a no-smoking range. They also countered many of Ben's claims about the degree of his own distress, with the result that the suit was dismissed. The effect was devastating on him. He spent the last six months of his sentence bitterly denouncing the CSC officials who, he claimed, gave false testimony at the trial.

It would be more accurate to say that the trial displayed the depressingly negative effect of antagonism between keeper and prisoner that beclouds the long history of the Big House in Kingston. Ben can be a perversely difficult person at times. He can also be open-hearted, good humoured, quick-witted, and dedicated to the task at hand. Few, if any, of the prison staff capitalized on his good qualities. The record of his incarceration, so far as I know it, is a record of a fruitless search for remedy by an unhealthy prisoner who, typically, received punishment instead.

At the end of his sentence in January 1997, and after a failed attempt by his lawyer to have the deportation order appealed, Ben, in ill-fitting clothes, was put on a plane to England with no money and no prospects. His life as a street person in London, waiting late into the night for charity vans that come round with leftovers from expensive hotel parties, is another and much longer story. Suffice it to say that the Canadian government has been more insensitive in this matter than the most hard-hearted keeper at the penitentiary.

Postscript: The Federal Court granted Ben's lawyer a hearing in late 1998 on the question of whether Ben should have the right to appeal his deportation. The claim was denied and Ben may remain in "exile" for the rest of his life.

AMOS'S STORY

Amos is a lifer no longer at K.P.; he now lives in a medium security jail. He came to my attention when he was editor of the newsletter published by the chaplaincy office. He is articulate, somewhat an activist by nature, sensitive to slights of any kind, small of stature, and distinctly uncomfortable when muscle is likely to be the deciding factor. His eyesight is so poor that he is technically blind. He enjoyed positions of trust at K.P., though he could never be accused of kowtowing to the administration.

Early in May of 1996, Amos delivered a paper message from the social development office to a particular range. The paper related to a fundraising activity planned by a group of inmates. One of the members of the group, believing that Amos was a mouthpiece for the hated social development office, set upon Amos and severely smashed his face. Amos was taken to a downtown hospital where he had bones reset, followed by plastic surgery to restore his face. Five days later he was returned to the prison hospital, still in much pain and badly swollen.

Amos reported that he was denied painkiller medication throughout the day of his return to K.P. until he demanded to be put in touch with his attending physician downtown. Later that evening he said he received Tylenol-3 and Demerol which brought him some relief from pain. He also learned that his cell on his home range had been assigned to someone else. He said he asked that the chaplain priest be brought to see him and that he, Amos, be allowed to use the telephone. The priest was not notified of the request and Amos was not allowed to use the phone until four days after his arrival at the prison hospital. His eyeglasses, without which he can scarcely see anything, his watch, clothes, and other personal effects were missing and could not be located.

A week after Amos's return to K.P. he still did not have his glasses and watch. They were returned to him a day later; that is, nine days after his return to the prison. The day after that, Amos was returned to a cell on his range where he lived until his transfer to a medium security jail.

A most distressing event in Amos's stay in the prison hospital was the death of an AIDS patient in a hospital cell nearby. He had been denied release by the parole board ten days earlier. Though the patient was monitored regularly by nursing staff during his final days, he was unattended at the time of his death. Hospital cells, like range cells, have barred gates allowing sounds of distress to carry all through the range. The priest was not called to comfort the dying prisoner and administer last rites. The cries of the man before he expired left Amos in misery and very angry at the prison staff. An incidental outcome was a recommendation from the jury of the coroner's inquest into the death of the man that a needle exchange program be set up in the prisons.

Enough of the Amos story has been told to make some observations. Medical treatment as provided at the K.P. hospital is minimally satisfactory. Most inmates with an aching tooth or a skin wound or an upset stomach are treated appropriately. In the 1995 inmate survey, 42 percent of maximum security inmates across Canada agreed with the statement "My non-emergency health problems have been taken care of."

Sometimes there is a serious delay in treatment. I recall seeing an inmate on a Thursday evening suffering, he claimed, from a bleeding ulcer. There was certainly a grey pallour in his face, and he left the meeting at least once to go the bathroom. I phoned the K.P. emergency number on Friday morning only to hear a recorded message, "This number is no longer in service." I called the nursing station and was told that the head of health services and the prison doctor were not expected to be in that day. The nurse said that there was no request for an appointment from that particular inmate. The fact is that the inmate's appointment for the previous Tuesday had been cancelled because of a lock-down whereby all inmates were confined to their cells. The following Wednesday, six days after I first saw his grey face, the inmate received ulcer medication.

The hospital is bright and the mood there is upbeat. The staff are well enough qualified and seem to like their work. What is missing is precisely what is missing everywhere in the Big House: a sense of care and concern about the emotional needs of the prisoner. Compassion can never flourish as long as the prisoner is regarded as a lesser being, as someone undeserving of humane treatment, as long as he is merely a "con." Deprived of the dignity accorded most other human beings, the prisoner acts out the stigma laid on him by his managers. It's an old story in the history of institutional management.

On May 11, 1998, there was a CBC News broadcast about a study just completed at Joyceville Penitentiary, Kingston, by Dr. Peter Ford, an AIDS specialist at the Kingston General Hospital. Dr. Ford described a sharp rise in the incidence of hepatitis C and a moderate rise in HIV at Joyceville. He found one third of the inmates were infected with hepatitis C; the incidence of HIV/AIDS among them was seventeen times higher than in the civilian population. Dr. Ford called it a major public health problem, considering that all of these men would be back on the street sooner or later and exposing others to their potentially deadly infectious diseases.

CBC News interviewed several inmates who talked freely about using dirty needles to get a "fix" and about unprotected sex among inmates. The warden said that condoms are available to inmates as well as bleach for sterilizing used needles. The head of health services for CSC said that a needle exchange for inmates has not been approved for security reasons. He conceded that the financial demands for improved security leave insufficient funds for treatment and prevention programs. The security staff, for their part, are not willing to undergo possible risk to their own safety nor to the safety of inmates resulting from a needle exchange. Dr. Ford concluded his interview by saying that if something isn't done, Canada will end up like the United States, where half the prison population (about half a million) are carriers of hepatitis C.

As a result of Dr. Ford's revelations, the *Financial Post* sent a reporter to K.P. who interviewed widely inside the institution.[52] She reported the view of one guard that 75 percent of inmates there test positive for either hepatitis C or HIV — no doubt a greatly exaggerated estimate. (Expert testimony puts the incidence of Hepatitis C at 33 percent of the Canadian prisoner population as compared with 0.5 percent of the civilian population.) The fear factor accounts for the reluctance of security staff to intervene in fights and their anxiety about being punctured by a needle stashed under a mattress.

The unions representing security staff in both the federal and provincial jails continue to resist efforts to provide a needle exchange. Advocates for prisoners, on the other hand, argue that the moral responsibility of the correctional services and their duty to provide health care require them to set up needle exchanges for addicted inmates. The Citizens Advisory Committee at K.P., on the initiative of one of its members, Carol Southall, a retired public health nurse, wrote a detailed letter in 1998 to the solicitor general of Canada recommending four policy changes in federal prisons:

1. Abolition of random urinalysis testing because of the cost of the program ($1,200,000 in 1995–96) and its counterproductive effects.
2. The introduction of methadone maintenance for hard-drug users in prison as a means of reducing illicit drug use and related criminal activity.
3. More aggressive drug treatment of hepatitis C cases.
4. A pilot needle exchange program based on recommendations from a variety of expert bodies, including the World Health Organization.

The nine-page letter caused a considerable flap within the upper structure of the Citizens Advisory Committees, where some people thought they had been blindsided by a local committee on important policy questions. The solicitor general replied that he would not authorize a needle exchange for prisoners.

It is apropos to repeat the acerbic observation of the *Financial Post* reporter — namely, that a sentence to prison should not be a sentence to death.

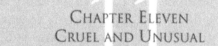

*In my opinion there is not one well-managed correctional
institution in North America. Not one. If ever the concept of
shared-governance should apply, it is in corrections. Presently,
because the public fear the stereotype of prisoners and won't
penetrate the taboo of prison and examine what they own and
maintain, prisons continue to be places where empires within
empires are born. In this kind of climate, any kind of
inhumanity can occur.*

   — J. Michael Yates, *Line Screw: My Twelve Riotous Years
     Working Behind Bars in Some of Canada's Toughest Jails*

The title of this chapter is taken without apology from Section
12 of the Canadian Charter of Rights and Freedoms:
"Everyone has the right not to be subjected to any cruel and
unusual treatment or punishment." "Everyone" includes, of course,
students in school, patients in a mental hospital, babies in an
abusive home, youngsters in a foster home and, yes, prisoners in a
jail. This book has documented casual abuse as the daily companion
of thousands of inmates of the Kingston Penitentiary since 1835.

A news story in the *Kingston Whig-Standard* dated June 22,
1991, comes to mind. It was entitled "AIDS Behind Bars." The

reporter talked with an HIV-infected inmate who wanted the outside world to know of his plight. He learned that he carried the HIV virus on the previous February 8th and freely admitted that he had threatened to spit and throw bodily fluids on staff who, after discovering that he was infected, harassed him. He was taken to the Hole (dissociation cells) on February 25, 1991, and kept there for five days. He said that guards verbally abused him by asking him when he was going to die and if he had killed his partner by giving him AIDS. On March 1, he was taken to an isolated cell in the prison hospital where he was still confined on June 22. He could not attend school nor any program. He said he received about an hour of exercise a week. Guards observed him on a video monitor.

The inmate's counsellor, a member of the Kingston AIDS Project, told the news reporter that the inmate was not dangerous as long as he was treated with a reasonable degree of compassion. The reporter observed that this prisoner was on a mission to break the taboos surrounding HIV/AIDS by candidly speaking out and by offering educational materials about the disease. I do not know the outcome of this story, but I can say with certainty that his claim of harassment by security staff rings true.

The stories that follow are from my own observations and recorded notes. They make it painfully clear that cruel and unusual punishment is still a feature of life inside Canada's Big House. Whereas cruel and unusual punishment in the nineteenth century was likely to be merely physical — for example, fifty strokes of the cat-o'-nine-tails energized by revenge — its meaning is much less clear now. Corporal punishment is *passé*, fortunately, in our prisons, schools and mental institutions. But some forms of psychological punishment — for example, confinement to the Hole at K.P. for six months or a year — is as much in the category of cruel and unusual punishment as the cat-o'-nine-tails. (As I write these lines I have learned that the Hole, that loathsome annex at K.P. built on the very same ground as the semi-underground prison for women back in the early days, is now closed and slated to be bulldozed out of existence.)

The root source of cruel and unusual punishment lies in the very nature of the human being — the high capacity of my species to treat others inhumanely; its frequent manifestation at K.P., as Michael Yates shouts out in *Line Screw*, is caused by the isolation of keepers and guards and prisoners from public scrutiny. The public relations people of the corrections system keep telling us that their operations are an open book, that their public accountability is a matter of great pride to them. Nothing could be more misleading.

A little context can throw some light on the inhumanity of the Kingston Penitentiary. Chapter 9 described the uncertainty of K.P.'s role since the great riot of 1971 — one step ahead followed by two steps back; a sideways slide and a lurch in the opposite direction; one warden after another till they are a blur in the memory; plans revealed and scrapped a season later. The only constant factors have been the noise of construction, the spending of money, and the flawed human relations among the people there.

One yardstick for measuring prison chaos is the frequency of lock-downs and subsequent stern measures. A lock-down has been, in recent times, the most evident "event" at K.P., mainly because the news media are usually notified when one occurs. Public notification allows a margin of time, often not enough, for appointments or visits with inmates to be cancelled or rescheduled. In many cases family visitors from faraway places have already arrived in Kingston, only to find they cannot have a visit after all — a painful and expensive inconvenience. (The latest administration at K.P., headed by Warden Monty Bourke, has worked energetically to reduce the frequency of lock-downs. But, alas, they still happen.)

A full lock-down means that inmates are locked in their cells for twenty-three hours a day until the cause of the emergency has been explored and remedies put in place. The prisoners are taken out in small batches for an hour of exercise in the yard or the gym. The visiting area, usually merry with the sounds of children, falls silent. Food preparation is done by staff standing in for convict kitchen workers. Meals are trundled on heavy steam carts to the floors of the wings; the meal trays are then carried to each prisoner inside his cell; all of this slows down "jug-up" time so severely that many do not receive their first meal of the day until noon and their second and final meal until 7 p.m. or even later. Emergency kitchen staff sometimes do not complete their clean-up until the early hours of the morning. Everybody, staff and inmates alike, pay the price for a lock-down.

There are partial lock-downs in less serious situations when the inmates are allowed their usual parade to the kitchen wickets for food trays and when family visits may continue. In any kind of lock-down, partial or complete, searches are often conducted for weapons, booze, and drugs. While a range search is under way, the inmates who live there are put under close guard in the gymnasium. The search teams enter every cell looking not only for bad stuff, but also for anything and everything not on the inmate's approved inventory. All such material is labelled either contraband or an unauthorized item and may be confiscated. In 1997, the warden tried to clear away the problem of widespread possession of contraband by declaring an amnesty day upon which a legal right of possession would come into force. As a result of endless "technical" problems, the amnesty never occurred and inmate cynicism about the system deepened.

One of my notes made in January 1994 states that as many as 232 inmates out of nearly 400 at K.P. were to be double-bunked until the sleeping ranges were all renovated. Given the fact that all of the federal jails were crowded then, the authorities had no alternative at K.P., it seems, but to cram two men into forty-five square feet of cell space while the old wings, one at a time, fell under the hammer of reconstruction. The hundred inmates lucky enough to be in C7, the K.P. "Hilton," had room enough for their two beds at floor level; as well, they were away from the racket and dust of construction in the main cell block.

The old cells that were refitted for double occupancy were equipped with a second bunk above the lower one. The bunks were sheets of steel welded to a frame. Each steel sheet was covered with a three-inch-thick fibre-fill mattress. The steel tended to whack and boing when a sleeping convict moved suddenly in the night. In the daytime, each occupant had to move sideways to navigate the length of the cell. There was a narrow bench table attached to the opposite wall that might contain a typewriter or computer and various personal effects. The prisoner working at the table had to sit hunched under the top bunk while the other one lay above him, reading or staring at the TV screen three or four feet from his face. When one of them used the toilet, he was in full view of the other one. The man using the top bunk had to get one foot on the bench in order to vault up top. To eat their meals, both men sat on the lower bunk with heads bent under the upper one. Cellmates who did not like each other were under nearly unbearable stress.

The Correctional Investigator of the Corrections Service said in his 1994–95 report, "Given the apparent ignoring of the issue at the national level, I feel it is necessary to once again restate the obvious; the housing of two individuals in a secure cell designed for one individual, for up to 23 hours a day for months on end is inhumane. This practice which continues unmonitored defies not only any reasonable standard of decency but also the standards of international convention."[53] The quotation is repeated for emphasis in the 1995–96 report wherein the investigator complained that he was still not getting any response from Corrections Canada on the matter. No wonder, then, that only 19 percent of maximum security inmates in the 1995 inmate survey agreed with the statement "I was generally satisfied with the Correctional Investigator's response to my complaint." The fault does not lie with the investigator.

Security staff at K.P, about 150 persons in 1994 out of a total staff in excess of three hundred, were also under much strain coping with unhappy prisoners and budget-cutting administrators. The exceptionally severe recession that swept the country in 1990 refused to go away quickly. Cutbacks became daily news, with the result that pay freezes for line staff were compounded by drastic reductions in overtime. Guards who had been on the overtime gravy train for years now found themselves unable to pay the bills for a lifestyle often too rich for their base incomes. The older guards resented green kids brought in on a casual basis as a way to deal with the overtime problem. The guards hammered this point home in the 1996 staff survey at K.P. Some of them viewed the dozen or more young women guards as next to useless in the K.P. environment.

A CHRONOLOGY OF RECENT EVENTS AT K.P. GLEANED FROM MY NOTEBOOKS:

ONE. In late October of 1993, the prison was locked down to permit a search of cells. On the third day of the lock-down, October 24, 1993, there was a lot of noisy complaining by convicts on Upper G range; it was 1 p.m. and they had not yet had their first meal. A black inmate named Robert "Tex" Gentles (his real name) had his radio turned up loud, as a form of protest, some said. There was a verbal confrontation with a guard(s) about the radio noise which led to the decision to move Tex to the Hole, the longtime favourite method for disciplining K.P. inmates. Soon after, Tex was dead.

Inmate Martens was locked in his cell on Lower G range that fateful Sunday. He routinely kept a journal of events from which an excerpt is reproduced as Appendix B at the back of this book. My own notes are the basis of the continuing account.

When Tex allegedly challenged the guards to come in and take him out of his cell, they responded to the challenge with alacrity. One of them was reported to have said to the prisoner, "We can do it the hard way or our way." (If the guards had simply allowed Tex to remain locked in his cell without electricity while he cooled down, he would still be alive). They requested from the deputy warden who was in charge of the jail that day a canister of Mace spray, a disabling tear gas which is propelled from its canister by Freon gas. The deputy sent the Mace to the guard in charge of the range. Several guards, including one woman, gathered to extract Tex from his cell. They directed at his head three squirts of Mace. He retreated to his wash basin to remove it from his face. (The MacGuigan report of 1977 recommended that tear gas never be sprayed on one inmate.)

The guard in the security cage at the end of the range unlocked the cell by remote control. Five guards squeezed and jostled their way into Gentles' cell and forced him down on his bunk in order to put cuffs on his wrists and walk him or carry him off to the Hole. (Tex was single bunked, a fact which permitted more guards to cram inside the cell and restrain him on his bunk). Once they got Tex down on his bed, the guards called for leg irons to stop him from kicking. While the leg irons were delivered, the guards applied pressure to Tex's upper body to keep him still. Neighbouring inmates stated that Tex was saying to the guards, "You don't have to do this," and "Stop kicking me."

With the leg irons attached, the guards commenced removing Tex from the cell. Inmates who could hear and/or see what was happening said they heard a guard say, "Give him another one." They also said that Tex appeared lifeless when he was brought out on the range. Some said that Tex was dropped on the stairway leading down to the lower level of the range. The guards put Tex inside the shower in the Hole in order to wash off the Mace as required by the rules. They reported to the deputy warden that the prisoner was in distress. A staff nurse was called to the Hole to attend to Tex. She later reported at the inquest that Gentles showed no vital signs while they awaited an ambulance to take him to a downtown hospital. In the emergency ward, he failed to respond to resuscitation.

During all of the proceedings on the range, the deputy warden, following long-established protocol, was not on the scene. The deputy warden, as the person in command of the prison that day, could, and almost certainly would have moderated the aggressiveness of the guards. Nearly five years later, in the course of testimony at the coroner's inquest, the then-deputy warden stated that the disabling gas, Mace, should not be used on an inmate in a controlled environment like a cell. It is a pity that he did not satisfy himself on that point on October 24,1993.

The post-mortem report by hospital physicians listed acute swelling of the trachea and bronchi, congestion of the lungs (consistent with the effects of Mace), swelling of the internal tissue of the neck consistent with external pressure on the neck, acute swelling of parts of the brain, a swollen lower lip with a cut inside, and acute congestion of the kidneys and spleen. The cause of death was reported as acute pulmonary congestion and oedema consistent with hypoxia, or asphyxiation. (Years later, the coroner's inquest produced forensic evidence that Gentles' face was held down in his pillow for as long as six minutes and possibly longer. Therefore smothering of the inmate by the guards was a possible cause of his death. Unfortunately, the provincial Attorney General's office did not have such forensic evidence when that office made the decision not to press criminal charges against any of the guards.)

The inquest was repeatedly delayed because of the possibility of criminal charges against some or all of the guards directly involved. After convoluted legal manoeuvres by the lawyers on both sides, charges were laid against two of the guards in a rare private prosecution and finally withdrawn by the Crown on grounds that the Crown prosecutor did not have sufficient evidence to proceed to trial. Four and a half years after Tex's death, on March 31, 1998, the coroner's inquest was finally commenced at Kingston with regional coroner Dr. Benoit Bechard in charge.

The *Kingston Whig-Standard* assigned a senior reporter to cover the inquest, which dragged on for more than a year. Public sessions with the jury present were held on 143 days, possibly the longest coroner's inquest on record. The room was half full of lawyers representing the variety of persons and institutions with standing and an interest in the outcome. Several months into the inquest, the lawyer for the Gentles family was able to get a court order widening the scope of the inquiry to include an investigation of the "subculture of violence" that allegedly permeated the ranks of the security staff at K.P. several years before the Gentles death. The result of this "diversion" was a detailed review of life inside the walls of K.P. in the 1990s.

On June 24, 1999, the jury reported its findings; this time, besides the lawyers, the other half of the room was filled with reporters, some of whom knew virtually nothing about the case as they watched the weary jury file in one last time.

Within minutes, those who had followed the inquest day by day heard the most significant decisions of the jury. They decided that Robert Wayne Gentles had died on his range — not in the Hole, not in the ambulance, not in the downtown hospital, but on his range. They decided that he had died of "asphyxia associated with multiple factors including the effect of Freon 113, restraint in a prone position, chest compression and suffocation." And, not least by any means, they decided that the cause of his death was an "accident."

Tex Gentles' mother, Carmeta, who took up temporary residence in Kingston in order to sit through the entire process, expressed her deep disappointment that the jury could conclude that her son's death was accidental. The guards concerned and the entire Corrections Canada community were relieved that the jury did not pronounce the awful word "homicide" as the cause of death. Everyone wondered if the book was closed in this case.

Without any accompanying analysis, the jury made seventy-four recommendations, cold turkey fashion. Some are merely procedural, while others point to fundamental changes at the Kingston Penitentiary and within Corrections Canada. Thirty-two of them — those that, in my opinion, bear directly on text in this book written before June 24, 1999 — are reproduced as Appendix C.

TWO. In December 1994, the inmates were unhappy over double bunking, food budget cutbacks, and other matters. Early in that month a lock-down was ordered that lasted about a week. My notebook contains few details of this incident; it is mentioned here merely as an indication of the dysfunctional state of the prison.

THREE. Fear of an epidemic of tuberculosis gripped the old jail in early 1995. Dr. Mary Pearson, the chief physician at the Prison For Women, as part of her inquiry into the prevalence of tuberculosis in Canadian prisons, conducted skin testing for TB at K.P. in late 1994. By January 12, 1995, she had determined that about one in every ten inmates at K.P. had come in contact with TB. That suggested to many that an epidemic existed or was imminent. Crowded and dusty conditions made matters worse, leaving the double-bunked inmates particularly vulnerable.

Skin testing, followed later by sputum sampling and chest X-rays under the supervision, at different times, of at least five doctors from various health jurisdictions, created an atmosphere of extreme anxiety. Early in February, Dr. Pearson was pulled off the inquiry at K.P. and replaced by Health Canada people. By the middle of February, the word was around that there were at least five active TB cases in the penitentiary, four of which were rumoured to be on the ranges. Exaggerated fears became the order of the day.

The prisoners refused to go to work under the misapprehension that they might be more exposed to TB outside their cells. The result was a self-imposed lock-down of sorts. Visits were allowed and inmate pay was extended even though no inmate work was done for several weeks. Prisoners who refused to be tested for TB were denied family visits. Early in March the prisoners' sit-down ended; the chest X-ray project dragged on until all five hundred had been bussed back and forth to the X-ray machine at a neighbouring jail. In the outcome, there were only a few active TB cases under care, all of which responded favourably to drug treatment.

FOUR. Each range has an elected range representative who acts as the link between the prisoners and their own inmate committee. The inmate committee, in turn, sits down with senior staff from time to time. By invitation, the reps met as a group with the citizens committee in early May of 1995, at which time there was an outpouring of complaints from all ranges. A sampling follows.

- Band practice time eliminated due to budget cuts affecting security staff.
- Common rooms meant for social and recreational purposes underutilized or not used at all.
- Tables removed from the ranges as a security measure, thereby making it more difficult to socialize on the ranges.
- Delays of thirty to forty minutes in arranging escorts to take prisoners to the visiting area to see family members.
- An escort now required for any inmate on the move around the yard, thus severely restricting freedom of movement.
- Inconsistency in the number of inmates able to be out of their cells and on a range at one time; sometimes only four, sometimes twice or three times that number, depending on the whim of the range security officer or the keeper on duty.
- People hired to conduct programs without adequate qualifications.
- Heightened tension as a result of increased urinalysis testing.
- Lack of recreational opportunities: "If you don't lift weights or play sports, you don't do nothing."

The inmate committee at that time was ineffective as a liaison with the warden; every committee either self-destructed after a few weeks because its members committed offences or the warden dissolved the committee in exasperation.

FIVE. In 1995, certain inmates in protective custody on Lower A range had heavy Plexiglas sheets placed over their cell gates to eliminate any risk of attack by a passing prisoner. The effect of the Plexiglas was to turn the cell into a stuffy cage where the inmate had to spend twenty-three hours out of twenty-four each day. The cages were, in effect, isolation prisons inside the segregation range inside the prison; a ghastly version of a Russian Easter egg.

SIX. In early November, 1995, the jail was locked down because the guards were conducting a work action (a work-to-rule of sorts) and the inmates were refusing to go to their jobs as long as the guards' action continued. This stand-off lasted more than a week.

SEVEN. Evidence of deteriorating conditions among the segregated inmates on A range was noted above. On Friday, December 22, 1995, an inmate on his twentieth day of a hunger strike was surviving on water and juices. The health service people stated that he was being monitored. Several segregated inmates reported that they were not getting their regulated one hour of exercise each day, that they were in their cells the full twenty-four hours. Health service told me that it was not a health issue(!) but a result of cutbacks to security staff. Anything can be rationalized in such an administrative structure.

Madam Justice Louise Arbour was the head of a 1995 *Commission of Inquiry into certain events at the Prison For Women in Kingston.* P4W, as it is known locally, opened in 1934, is across the road from the Kingston Penitentiary; the reader will recall how the history of the two prisons is intimately intertwined.

The Arbour Report[54] was a launching pad for a blistering criticism of Corrections Canada for wantonly flouting the law regarding the segregation of federal inmates. Justice Arbour wrote, "There is no rehabilitative effect from long-term segregation, and every reason to believe it may be harmful. I realize that there are circumstances where segregation, even prolonged segregation, may be inevitable. I see no alternative to the current overuse of prolonged segregation but to recommend that it be placed under the control and supervision of the courts." That recommendation has never been adopted. Too cumbersome and too fraught with lawyers — those were two of the reasons why the recommendation was stillborn. However, there were "consequences" after the publication of the report. Commissioner John Edwards resigned and the entire system has inclined itself in the direction of better compliance with the law.

EIGHT. The old segregation unit — the Hole — was unusually cold in January of 1996. It was explained that the work of the retro-fit had temporarily interrupted the normal heat flow to that area. Nevertheless, all the cells in the Hole were full. Inmates wrapped themselves in their blankets as they sat or lay watching their little TV screens.

NINE. In the fall of 1995, the recreation officer reluctantly agreed with me to allow two college and university sports teams into the institution for a series of "exhibition" games against prisoner teams. Only one game of basketball was played in the late fall, at which there were no more than ten inmate spectators, those who happened to be on the weight-lifting gallery at the time. The reason given was that the inmates were not interested in watching a sports event after supper. In truth, the event was not publicized and only one ethnic group, four hours before the event, was invited to field players. It was near the end of February 1996, before any more games were played because the inmate sports supervisors were segregated in the Hole in late January in connection with an incident. The recreation officer said that he could not conduct games without his inmate sports commissioner. The inmates would not likely play, he said, if he, the recreation officer, picked the team! The games with the visiting students ended in March and were never resumed even though the students were willing to return. The failed effort to engage outsiders in sports events at K.P. gives new meaning to the old army expression SNAFU: Situation Normal, All Fucked Up.

TEN. On Monday, April 29, 1996, a new warden arrived at K.P. That night, the correctional supervisor in charge of security happened to be a person with a reputation for aggressive management. When a small group of inmates on H range refused to return to their cells at lock-up time, the Emergency Response Team was fitted up in their black gear, plastic shields, batons, and heavy boots and ordered onto ranges where minor disorder had been reported. Towards 11 p.m., the mandatory video camera showed the team entering Upper H. All inmates were in their cells and gates were being locked. The team then went to Upper A range. The camera filmed the team as they approached two inmates from behind. The prisoners appeared to be walking towards their cells. The team seized them, slammed them down on the floor, and put restraints on them. They were taken to the Hole, where their clothes were cut off and they were placed naked inside bare cells.

The team returned to Upper H and proceeded to extract from his cell a noisy inmate who had just slashed himself. Blood was evident in the video picture. The inmate was Maced (gassed) and forcibly removed to the Hole, where he too was stripped and placed in a cell with no bed clothing. A nurse tried without success to attend to the cut on his arm while he cursed the staff as racist bastards. He was left alone.

The Team returned to Upper H to extract an intoxicated inmate from his cell. His clothes were cut off as the video camera looked on dispassionately. To perform that operation, the shackled inmate was put face down on the floor. A guard quickly slit through the clothing, up each leg from heel to waist, thence a final slit to the inmate's collar. His clothes fell away like the skin from a rabbit. He went naked and without protest to the dome area, where he was outfitted with a paper gown for the short walk to the shower stall in the Hole. He was left in the shower stall for the night, there being no other space for him. The prison doctor sutured the cut on the arm of the self-wounded inmate, who continued to protest that he had been mistreated and abused. By now, he had a mattress on his bed. The video camera picked up the sounds of another inmate in the Hole who was apparently drunk and very foul-mouthed. The video record ended shortly after 1 a.m. The institution remained locked down for several days while a search was conducted for booze and weapons.

There was an internal investigation of the events of April 29 to determine whether the actions of the Emergency Response Team were warranted and, indeed, whether the decision to call in the team was based on any real threat to security. As a result, several officers were reprimanded or fined, or both. Conditions in the Hole were improved by the new warden, Jim Blackler, such that inmates there would get their toiletries and bedding promptly, all cells would be equipped with an electric outlet (some had none), and all inmates in the Hole would have access to a phone. The use of the Emergency Response Team would be limited to serious situations of disruption, negotiation to be the preferred alternative. The head of the prison would henceforth be on the scene during ERT actions.

The effect of the events of April 29, 1996, lingered on for many months at K.P. Some said the officers on duty that night wanted to show the new warden their muscle power. The entire exercise was reminiscent of the "subculture of violence" identified in the Day/Rees report back in 1989. An important difference lay in the fact that by 1996 the ERT members were well disciplined and thoroughly efficient in carrying out their task. But they lacked the discretionary power needed to flex with a changing situation. The team was trained to perform a physical force routine to its final completion and without the slightest modification unless ordered otherwise by the prison manager. What was needed, obviously, was a requirement that the prison manager be present while the team was in action.

ELEVEN. In early June, 1996, an inmate was beaten with a baseball bat inside the washroom in the prison yard. Seventy inmates in the yard refused to go back to their ranges. The use of the Emergency Response Team was threatened. The rebels agreed to go back to their cells in batches of ten. The victim of the beating was taken to hospital downtown. There was a partial lock-down of the jail for several days while the beating was investigated.

TWELVE. In the middle of February 1997, K.P. was locked down to permit a search for a weapon or weapons that might have been used in the stabbing of an inmate. The lock-down continued for a week.

THIRTEEN. In mid-March 1997, a member of the Citizens Advisory Committee reported that she saw many, many cockroaches skittering on the shelves and tables of the prison kitchen. I telephoned all three prison kitchen numbers with no answer at any of them. A call to Health Canada in Kingston to find out if there was a routine inspection of federal prison eating facilities activated an answering machine. Several hours later a senior administrator at K.P., obviously informed of my message on the Health Canada answering machine, severely upbraided me for not consulting him about the cockroaches; he said that there could not be a problem because the kitchen was regularly sprayed for vermin and that the kitchen was inspected twice a year. The next day, I reached the Health Canada official in Kingston, who said that, because of cutbacks, he was alone in the office and unable to take phone calls when they came in. He said that he would sometimes do an inspection of a prison kitchen but never in detail because he did not have time. I asked if, in effect, corrections officials do their own inspections of prison kitchens and he said partly so. In the outcome, there was a prompt inspection of the kitchen at K.P. by health officials.

FOURTEEN. During the first week of June, 1997, the jail was locked down as a result of a stabbing incident.

FIFTEEN. In early July 1997, a prisoner on Upper H range ran amok and single-handedly broke all the lower windows, twisted some metal window frames, ripped down murals on newly redecorated walls, and pulled the heat radiators loose from their moorings, releasing a flood of water onto the range and down the stairwell to the floor of the Dome. According to some accounts, he also damaged the range fridge and microwave. After some three hours of rampage, the offender was taken by the Emergency Response Team to the Hole. The windows and heat radiators were not repaired until October. Mosquitoes and flies freely toured the range throughout the summer. The frosty nights of early autumn tested the endurance of the occupants of that range. Prison officials said that the window replacement material took a long time to fabricate. Two or three questions can be asked here but will never be answered. Was the rampaging prisoner deliberately allowed to carry on for three hours in order to shock the warden into a more sympathetic attitude towards the security staff? Would broken windows in a senior administrator's office have taken four months to repair - or even four days?

SIXTEEN. Late August, 1997. A number of guards entered the same range (Upper H) to deal with an inmate in distress. Other inmates refused to return to their cells. There was a confrontation in the course of which a guard was struck and knocked down by an inmate with a broomstick. After the wounded officer was removed from the range, the turbulence on the range escalated into a miniriot. Fires were set. Various pieces of hardware were used to barricade the entry gate to the range. The Emergency Response Team, supported by negotiators, finally restored order on the range by 5 a.m. An internal investigation was completed and a few inmates were charged with criminal offences.

On September 10, a member of the Citizens Advisory Committee toured Upper H range in the company of a correctional supervisor. The CAC member reported some appalling conditions on the range:

- The floor was flooded deep enough to soak the trouser cuffs of the escort.
- Garbage was scattered around and some inmates complained of garbage in their cells that had not been collected.
- A number of inmates had no bedding or mattresses and had been cold during the night because of the broken windows (from the one-inmate rampage dating back to early July).
- Inmates on special diets for reasons of religion or allergies were not receiving their special diets.
- Many inmates said they had not showered in four days and that no laundry was being done

- Overall, the range was quiet, though tension was high.

Nine months later, at least one of the offenders from Upper H was still in the Hole awaiting disposition of his case. So much for the thirty-day maximum specified in the CCRA!

Partly as a result of the troubles on Upper H, the atmosphere of the prison deteriorated noticeably. The security staff made demands on the warden for better protection in managing inmates while on their ranges. The guards insisted that the inmates had to lock themselves inside their cells before any officer entered a range for the hourly walk. The inmates responded that a minimum number should be allowed to remain on the ranges during walks by the guards — those, for example, having a shower or talking on the telephone. Union-management discussions went on for many weeks before the security staff were even minimally satisfied on the safety issue. Throughout these negotiations, the level of civility steadily deteriorated.

SEVENTEEN. In late September of 1997, there was a complete lock-down again. The guards appeared to be tense, insecure, and punitive in their attitude. Many of the prisoners were abusive and challenging in the way they spoke. Some prisoners were allowed to pick up their own food trays and others were not. Some who could do so refused to join the "jug-up" line until others were allowed to do the same. On Monday, September 29, the inmates on Upper H, still with broken windows and no heat radiators, had not yet been fed at 2 p.m.

EIGHTEEN. In December, 1997, a new warden and management team arrived for the purpose of restoring calm and civility to the institution. The departing warden appeared to be the fall guy for a breakdown in union-management relations. The new team's vigorous efforts to restore harmony and the evident change for the better in the prison's atmosphere gave some hope for the future of K.P.

NINETEEN. This final entry shows how cruel and unusual treatment of convicts can reach beyond the expiry of a sentence, beyond the walls of the prison, and into the private lives of many people on the street. Seth's story (not his real name) makes the disturbing point that men and women in power in Canada can just as casually violate the rights of an individual for the collective good, as they see it, as any of the tyrants of history whom we revile in the classrooms and pulpits of the nation.

Seth, an aboriginal Canadian, served nine years in federal penitentiaries for serious sex offences in Saskatchewan. He is exceptionally intelligent, high-spirited, witty, and gregarious. While in jail he took part in escapades, some of them serious, that got him into difficulties with Corrections Canada, and for which he was duly penalized. Instead of being released under supervision at the halfway or two-thirds point of his sentence, he was detained to the end of his sentence and sent into the community without any support system whatever.

He had, indeed, followed his correctional plan quite well; programs completed included The Native Holistic Program, Alternatives to Violence (first and second level), Cognitive Skills Training, Anger Management, and the Substance Abuse Treatment Program. He did not fully complete the Sex Offender Treatment Program because his participation was interrupted by a transfer within the system. He spent some time in the Special Handling Unit (SHU), taking part of the rap, he told me, for a friend who had assaulted a guard. He came out of the SHU bearing the stigma "Extremely Dangerous," a label that does not square with the comments of his program instructors. But it was enough to persuade the parole board to detain him to the end of his sentence.

The local police visited Seth just before his release date in October 1997; the police told him he would not be welcome in Kingston. He said that he would be moving on. Once outside the walls, he went to a friend's place in a small town seventy-five miles away. There they noisily celebrated his release from prison. The friend also had an apartment in Kingston to which they returned in a week's time.

Seth had thereby broken his undertaking to stay away from Kingston. The Kingston and Toronto police, following established procedures, released to the newspapers a set of details designed to show that Seth was an extremely dangerous sex offender. The *Kingston Whig-Standard* ran a story and picture on the front page under the headline "High-Risk Offender Makes City Home." A reader would not find any redeeming qualities in the character described in the story.

Immediately after the newspaper publicity, Seth was subjected to a rat-tat-tat of persecution and harassment in Kingston by the police, the Kingston Housing Authority, which owned the building where he stayed, and by various private individuals. The city warned him that he would be treated as a trespasser at any of their housing units. Police surveillance was constant. On November 12, a car in which he was riding in the city was pulled over by the police. Everyone was required to get out and describe their activities and destinations. On November 18, Seth was summoned to police headquarters, where he ran a gauntlet of uniformed officers, to be later confronted by the senior officers, who pressed the point that he was expected to leave town right away. On November 29, he was overtaken by a small group of foul-mouthed men outside a drinking establishment in Kingston and beaten very severely with a bat.

He managed to get to the place where he had temporary shelter. Next morning he could not move because of terrible pain. He was taken to the Kingston General Hospital, where it was found that a broken rib had punctured a lung, allowing the lung to fill up with blood. Seth was placed in the intensive care unit while a pump slowly removed the offending matter from his lung.

Seth did not leave the hospital until January 8, 1998. The exterior wall of his damaged lung became badly infected, requiring major surgery on December 29. The lung had to be lifted out so that its entire outer covering could be scraped away. When he left the hospital, he was taken into a friendly aboriginal household for a long and uncertain recuperation. By the third week of January, Seth was well enough to take some exercise and eat more heartily. Around the middle of January, police surveillance ceased. He began to lead a normal life in the company of aboriginal friends.

On June 24, 1998, I learned that the Ontario Provincial Police had recently tracked Seth to his home in a rural place and advised him that steps were being initiated that might place him in the Dangerous Offender category, leading, possibly, to reimprisonment for the rest of his life. To the best of my knowledge, there were no new offences behind this action, but merely the conviction of Corrections Canada and the police that Seth did not belong in civil society.

The *Kingston Whig-Standard* reported on July 7, 1998, that Seth was arrested for beating and sexually assaulting a woman on June 30 in Kingston. As this is being written, he has been in custody for eleven months waiting for a trial date. The delay relates to the failure of the Crown prosecutor to disclose to Seth's lawyer the full facts surrounding the arrest in 1998. The mills of the gods do indeed grind slow and exceedingly fine.

The bill for Seth's hospitalization would have been at least fifteen thousand dollars and possibly twice as much, paid by the taxpayers of Ontario. That is merely the most obvious cost of the disastrous decision by the Kingston Penitentiary and the police departments of at least two cities to let loose the hounds of retribution on a person who showed signs of improvement while still in prison. He should have been released into the community before warrant expiry while supervision was still possible. And if the parole board lacked the courage to do that, corrections officials had a duty to Seth, as to any other released prisoner, to plug a gaping hole in corrections policy and see that community support was available. What was done instead was the opposite of what Canadians take for granted in their free country.

Seth's story highlights the flaws in the risk assessment business in which case management officers in federal prisons engage themselves every day. A professor of criminology at Carleton University in Ottawa, Dr. Maeve McMahon, speaks of it as the "McDonaldization" of corrections.[55] If you want efficient service, a familiar menu, standard pricing, and cheery surroundings, you go to the fast food chain of your choice. Somewhat in the same way, a prison official, using numerical values, tallies up the numbers for the original crime, the prison programs taken, the age/sex of the offender, the offences while incarcerated, etc., and comes up with a numbered risk factor that renders the inmate not dangerous, somewhat dangerous, or extremely dangerous. The case management officer can do all of this without getting to know the individual except in the most superficial way. Some prisoners at K.P. have said that they do not know the name of their CMO (now called a parole officer) and cannot remember the last time they met. In the 1995 inmate survey, of one thousand maximum security inmates who answered the question, 24 percent said they had never met their CMO and another 33 percent said, "A few times a year."

The opening words of this chapter were those of J. Michael Yates, the poet and academic who chose the life of a prison guard for twelve years in his late adult life. "If ever the concept of shared governance should apply, it is in corrections."[56] Most of the incidents described above would never have happened if the jail had been under the benign and careful scrutiny of a public board made up of persons sensitive to the needs of incarcerated men. For one thing, the quasi-military structure passed down through the generations would have been replaced long ago by more democratic arrangements whereby small groups of prisoners would share with staff the planning for work and play and education.

There is emerging evidence that democratic principles are being applied with good results in the lower security jails. In some of them, the staff are indistinguishable in dress from convicts. They speak to each other using first names. They enjoy each other's company. They quietly go about the business of making the world a better place. It is hard to imagine such a revolution at the Kingston Penitentiary. Most of the staff would say it's impossible with that bunch of losers. In spite of that, the current team of senior administrators at K.P., in the space of a few months, had changed the atmosphere for the better. Can they reverse the tide of history at the Big House?

CHAPTER TWELVE
WHITHER THE BIG HOUSE?

O ver the last several chapters I have documented an implicit claim that the Kingston Penitentiary has become dysfunctional and therefore obsolete during the second century of its life.

Kingston Penitentiary as seen across Portsmouth Harbour, 1999.

Like many old prisons, its physical design is impractical for the kind of social interaction and rehabilitative leadership needed for modern corrections. Putting sixty-five men on one range, most of them socially disadvantaged, without meaningful work, without vocational training opportunities, without any significant role in planning their personal lives, with meagre and uninspired recreational experiences, with the TV set and cigarettes as their main diversion, with a gut craving for the excitement of a family visit or some secretly stashed brew — that is a recipe for failure in human and correctional terms.

The leadership of the Canadian correctional service know this perfectly well. That is why the newer and lower security jails for both men and women are radically different in design. Typically, they feature groupings of a dozen prisoners in a living unit under inmate management and with ample opportunities for recreation, education, and training. The Kingston Penitentiary is captive to a physical layout meant for isolating and punishing large numbers of people in the cheapest possible manner. It grants less dignity to maximum security inmates than to other inmates. The most needful get the least service. The inmate survey of 1995 garnered 53 percent agreement among minimum security inmates that "CSC offers enough programs to meet my needs" — an unimpressive response by any standard. Of the 928 maximum security inmates who answered the question, a mere 24 percent agreed!

The long history of stigmatizing and demeaning the prisoner at K.P. has affected the mentality of corrections staff there, easily outweighing any enlightenment brought into the system by the younger staff with their diplomas or degrees in sociology and criminology. Those confined at K.P. have always been "cons" without redeeming qualities and without first names.

Until very recently, a guard who wanted the attention of Chris, for example, would bawl down the range "Jones!!" loud enough to be heard out on King Street. And Jones would reply in a surly voice "Yeah, Copper — whaddya want?" A visitor could never be sure whether this kind of bawling back and forth was merely "friendly" banter or deep-seated hostility. Security officers now use walkie-talkies to contact the range officer who, in turn, calls the message to the inmate in quieter and more civil terms. For the hourly range walk by the guard, the "cons" must be caged; that is, locked in their cells, to prevent any unprovoked attack or attempt at hostage taking. The uniformed figure who walks past the barred gates is, with exceptions, of course, the enemy who, in return, views the prisoners as scum.

As the twentieth century ends, the prevailing mantra both in the public and private domains is "downsizing." Computer technology has made it possible to replace tens of thousands of workers in service and processing industries, both in the private and public sectors. The displaced workers and managers struggle to find new niches or invent new opportunities. Though unemployment in Canada remains stubbornly high, at around 8 percent, wealth creation grows and government revenues are buoyant — just now, anyway. Thanks in part to downsizing, public budgets are being balanced and debts are being managed.

Across North America, and particularly in the United States, there is one industry that resists downsizing: the corrections industry. Like Topsy, it just grows. The surface reason is obvious: more people are being sent to jail each year and fewer are being released as soon as they should be. Corrections Canada publishes a neat little pocket book of data each year that confirms this trend.

Beneath the surface is the disturbing fact of a functionally illiterate minority marginalized by the communications revolution. Living by their wits, many of them run afoul of the law and get sent to jail. There is a recent newspaper story of a woman given six months in jail for cheating on the welfare system. Her lawyer argued unsuccessfully that sentencing her to a period of community work would be better than jailing her. The prosecutor countered with the revealing rejoinder that the integrity of the welfare system relies on the deterrent effect of a jail sentence more than on intrusive methods such as spying to catch the cheats.[57] This case supports the contention of authors such as Ruth Morris and Linda McQuaig that prisons are now an occasional repository for the permanently unemployed.

That is why, one could argue, K.P. was not converted into a museum long ago. It is a workable maximum security jail. Also, the walls enclose a regional treatment centre for criminals who need short-term psychological treatment. Many of the maximum security types at K.P. are there because the other jail managers don't want them. These, then, are the detritus of the Ontario federal prison population. With prison beds at a premium, the senior planners must have a secure place for the flotsam and jetsam of the system. That is the current mandate of the Kingston Penitentiary.

Though flawed by a paint-by-numbers methodology, the security classification process, so frequently sought by nineteenth century humanitarians, has resulted in an array of medium and minimum security jails feeding into scores of community corrections facilities on quiet streets across the country. In the outcome, many prisoners successfully cascade downwards to freedom and a new life of social responsibility. They can be compared to the beneficiaries of the letter grade system in school. Those who get boosted from Cs to straight As are psychologically rewarded and are given a leg-up for the rest of their lives. But those who cannot or will not get out of the morass of Ds and Fs are failures and no-goods in their own eyes and everyone else's. They are the current inhabitants of K.P.

It surely is the supreme irony in the history of the jail that the very classification system urged for so long by chaplains and enlightened wardens a hundred years ago has vouchsafed the reputation of the institution as a sinkhole. After nearly 175 years, it houses the Ds and the Fs of the Canadian prison population: the "worst" of the sex offenders and murderers, the least educable, the least reconcilable, the most godforsaken, the most hated.

It is no surprise, therefore, that convicts will go to almost any lengths to avoid being sent to K.P. Worse, by far, than the mark of Cain is the mark of K.P. in your record. In May of 1999 the news media went wild over a sensational escape from the old jail. A professional bank robber named Tyrone Conn broke K.P's forty-year record without escapes. Depressed by his failure to gain a transfer to a medium security prison, he hatched a plan to go over the thirty-foot wall. Critical to the plan was a ladder, a grappling hook, and material that could serve as a rope, all of which he scrounged in the canvas shop where he worked.

On the chosen day, instead of returning to the main cell block after work, Conn hid himself in the canvas shop and waited for the onset of night, necessarily a moonless night. With luck and a lot of physical dexterity, he moved his makeshift ladder, hook, and rope to a secluded part of the east wall. Within minutes, he was up and over to freedom without ever being detected by the security staff of the prison. He paid a brief visit to his mother in a nearby city, stole a car, robbed a bank, and made his way to Toronto. A little over two weeks later, holed up in the basement apartment of a former girlfriend and surrounded by police, Conn shot himself with a stolen gun. The fatal shot came in the middle of a conversation with a CBC television producer who was trying to talk him into giving himself up. He would not be returning to K.P.

A purely expedient reason for the old jail's continuing effort to remain viable is the size of recent capital spending inside the walls. As noted in Chapter 8, I asked the deputy commissioner (Ontario) by letter for the record of capital expenditures at K.P. since 1971. Four months and several phone calls later, he replied that capital budget details are destroyed after seven years and that, therefore, he could only supply capital spending information for the last seven years. In the outcome, though I asked for the last seven years, I received information for the last four and a half years. In Chapter 8 I offered evidence that upwards of a hundred million dollars have been spent fixing up the place since the great riot of 1971. That is quite separate from the operating costs, which are now running between $60,000 and $70,000 per inmate per year. That figure is in stunning contrast to $450 per year per prisoner at the beginning of this century. As recently as 1977, the average cost per male federal inmate across Canada was $17,515. That average figure had grown to $50,375 by 1997.[57]

The cost in the late 1990s to educate a child in the publicly supported schools of Ontario is approximately $7,000 a year. After allowing for the cost of room and board, it seems absurd on the face of it to be spending nine times that amount to keep prisoners in an obsolete institution like the Kingston Penitentiary. The absurdity would be less striking if there was more evidence of reclamation and rehabilitation of those who live there.

They are an aging inmate population at K.P.; the average age is about 45. They become old in appearance and condition in their mid-fifties. The old ones suffer from a variety of ailments, such as liver and kidney disease, AIDS, arthritis, cancer, and Parkinson's disease. A high percentage of them are lifers with no chance of parole for fifteen or more years. Some will never be paroled; they will die there.

In the never-ending talk about changing the system to make it more workable, there was a tentative plan a few years ago to convert the Prison For Women into a geriatric unit for male prisoners. The plan was shelved when CSC could not figure out how to empty P4W of its female occupants. There are still a couple of dozen maximum security and high-need psychiatric cases rattling around inside the Prison For Women with a staff twice or three times as numerous as the inmates.

A former K.P. inmate passed on to me an idea for a community-based hostel for old male prisoners. Such persons as these, he thought, should be eligible for admission:

- ex-prisoners who have completed their sentence but have no family or accepting community;
- prisoners over 65 with terminal illnesses;
- wheelchair-bound prisoners;
- prisoners over 55 who were convicted of sex crimes and who are at risk of having their names and crimes publicized in any community they might try to enter;
- prisoners who require long-term daily nursing care; and
- prisoners of any age with confirmed AIDS.

A hostel for aging and dying prisoners fits nicely into the recycling ethic we now embrace. A closed hospital, for example, with its various treatment facilities, could easily be converted into a nursing home, not only for old prisoners, but for others as well. Prisoners who continue to be a demonstrable threat to society could hardly be admitted to such a facility; most older prisoners, however, are not in that category. All of them would benefit immeasurably from more community contact.

Substantial cost savings would come from placing old prisoners in a facility with sophisticated care arrangements. It now costs Corrections Canada a minimum of $700 a day to place an inmate in a hospital in downtown Kingston. In addition, there is the extra cost of posting a guard outside the room twenty-four hours of the day. My ex-inmate contact says that nursing home care could be provided for about $20,000 per capita per year in contrast to the $50,000 to $70,000 tab at the penitentiaries. It is difficult to know if his estimate is sound. I think he underestimates the security cost factor needed to reassure an anxious public.

In any event, it will take a long time for public opinion to soften on the matter of the effectiveness of our jails. A large majority of voters feel good about sending lawbreakers to jail; the worse the crime, the longer the time. What the social scientists already know — that there is no correlation between the number of people in jail and the crime rate — has not made the least dent in popular thinking. Scientists in Finland, for example, learned long ago that the percentage of drunk drivers sent to jail could be reduced from 80 percent to 20 percent without having any apparent effect on the frequency of drunk driving. Factors other than imprisonment have reduced drunk driving in that country.[59] A study of incarceration rates and crime rates in the 1980s in the United States revealed that while the imprisonment rate in North Dakota, as a matter of conscious public policy, was half that of South Dakota, the crime rate in the two neighbouring states remained about the same.[60]

In the variety of efforts to reclaim prisoners at K.P., there are some successes to report, of course. Isolated individuals on the staff go about their work with an evident sense of mission and surprising good will. They are shining lights and deserve more recognition than they get.

The school at K.P. clunks along in a modest way. It has been recently moved to the former photocopying shop. (What would the managers of K.P. do without all that unused shop space from the nineteenth century?) The school is conducted under a private contract with an outfit called Excalibur. There are about a dozen teachers, full or part time, serving 120 inmates the last time I asked. Ninety of those were doing basic upgrading to grade ten; the remaining 30 at the school were taking high school credits or Seneca Community College credits. Nearly 250 of the prison population of four-hundred-plus do not have grade ten standing. The school is an oasis of friendly quietness. Its camouflaged walls conceal the pain of hard labour done there many long years ago. The frequent lock-downs leave an observer wondering how the teachers ever reach their curriculum objectives.

Tucked away in various nooks and crannies are programs and programs and programs, just like the menu at McDonalds. Corrections Canada boasts an annual expenditure of 120 million dollars on programs for prisoners across the country.[58] Some are specifically designed for aboriginal offenders; others, for sex offenders, substance abusers, wife beaters, etc. Some are given by persons especially contracted for a particular program. Most are given by CSC staff. The shorter the prisoner's term, the more likely he will get the program of his choice. The operating principle is that a recommended program must be taken close to parole eligibility date. If a man is doing a life sentence with no parole for twenty years, he is not going to get into a program to address his criminogenic needs, as the jargon goes, until he has forgotten what those needs were.

The inmate survey of 1995 roundly denounced the timing of programs in the federal jails. Across all security levels, between 78 percent and 80 percent agreed that "programs should be offered early in a sentence instead of just prior to release."

The approximately 150-plus lifers at K.P., generally speaking, rehabilitate themselves. They "mellow out" as the years go by; they lose their anger, perform their trivial work quietly, and hope for a trailer visit with a family member. They watch TV, smoke a lot, and become unhealthy.

The Lifers Group, with a membership floating up and down around forty, was until recently the most stable group at K.P. In addition to a social meeting once a week with outside volunteers, the Lifers illustrated that constructive rehabilitative work can be done by inmates themselves. Each November, the Lifers conducted a Prisoners Information Day at which the warden, sympathetic politicians, and prisoner advocates expressed their views with candour. The Lifers have also had some success in offering peer counselling on an organized basis. From time to time they have tried to prevent suicides and have worked to reduce disease and infection from such activities as tattooing, sexual contact, and shooting up with dirty needles. The beneficial work of the Lifers has declined of late in keeping with the general deterioration of the prison population.

The Native Brotherhood is an eclectic mix of prisoners from a variety of aboriginal nations in North America. Their membership is sometimes leavened by other second-class citizens who have no Native blood. The Brotherhood has fostered an appreciation of Native ways of thinking, praying, and healing both within staff and inmate ranks. Once a month, they hold a sweat lodge on a tiny patch of "sacred" ground behind the shops. Anyone lingering beside Portsmouth harbour at sweat lodge time can see wood smoke rising above the wall and hear poignant chanting to the insistent beat of a drum.

Taking programs and going to school constitute work and, therefore, the enrollees get paid the same as those few who work in the various shops and clean the floors and yards. The pay varies from five to seven dollars a day, enough to afford tobacco and sundries from the canteen. Those who buy a computer or designer clothes or fancy footwear or who pay tuition for a university course use extra money donated by a relative or friend. Nobody has cash, at least legally. Their money is held in trust by the institution and therefore can only be spent by means of a paper transaction through the authorities.

Many of these closing words have been about money — about the high cost of running this institution. But a balanced assessment of the utility of K.P. must get beyond the issue of money. The text above has repeatedly demonstrated the heartlessness of Canada's Big House. Despite all the efforts of exceptional persons since 1835, including the present warden Monty Bourke, to bring the healing power of mutual respect into the jail, the prevailing climate is hostile. It cannot be otherwise, given the weight of history and the power of peer pressure.

An approach to lifting K.P. out of its arid hostility syndrome and onto the green pasture of mutual respect may lie in the field of governance. The coroner's jury in the Gentles case, having listened to a long parade of witnesses for more than a year, concluded that more civilian oversight of Corrections Canada and all its parts is necessary. The jury was not specific beyond saying that an independent oversight committee should be set up by the Solicitor General of Canada to study the problem and report within a year. I will be surprised if such a study is conducted. The politicians, typically, think that the chain of public accountability up the line to Parliament is strong and effective. They also think that it would be bad policy to do anything that might strengthen the hand of the convict population and thereby heighten public fears.

The contrary point of view, and presumably that of the Gentles jury, is that public safety can be enhanced by having effective civilian review of the day-by-day operations of the prisons so that there can never again be the kind of abusive, secretive, arbitrary, and discriminatory treatment of prisoners of the kind repeatedly documented in the foregoing pages.

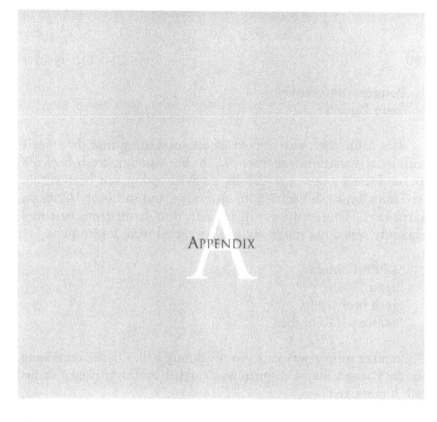

This is a typed version of the original handwritten meal schedule, with commentary added.

Diet Table of Convicts at the Provincial Penitentiary
1st October 1836

BREAKFAST Sunday
Bread 1/2 lb.
Fresh Beef 1/3 lb.
Potatoes 1/40 bushel
Coffee 1 pint
Molasses 1/4 gill (a gill is just over half a cup)

The same breakfast was served on the remaining six days with minor variations (no meat on Monday, fresh beef 3/8 lb. on Tuesday, salt pork 3/8 lb. on Wednesday, no meat on Thursday, fresh beef 3/8 lb. on Friday and salt beef 1/2 lb. on Saturday).

DINNER Sunday
Bread 1/2 lb.
Fresh beef 1/3 lb.

Potatoes 1/40 bushel
Soup 1 quart

The same diet was offered at all succeeding mid-day meals with meat variation (salt beef 1/2 lb. on Monday, fresh beef 3/8 lb. on Tuesday, salt pork 3/8 lb. on Wednesday, salt beef 1/2 lb. on Thursday, fresh beef 3/8 lb. on Friday, and salt beef 1/2 lb. on Saturday). The soup would be different from time to time. Quantity was quite stable but quality varied from fair to poor.

SUPPER Sunday
Bread 3/8 lb.
Fresh beef 1/3 lb.
Potatoes 1/40 bushel

Sunday supper was eaten in the dining hall. On the remaining six days (work days), supper was carried by the prisoner to his cell. It consisted of:

Porridge 1 quart
Molasses 1/4 gill

Typically, the porridge was made from cornmeal. Prisoners were allowed a piggen (a small bucket) of water each day, which they carried to their cells.

APPENDIX B

Here are two excerpts from the journal of the so-called "Prison Violence Project," a copy of which was given to the author as chairman of the Citizens Advisory Committee at K.P. The project was headed by inmate Rudolf "Rudy" Martens, assisted by inmate Joe Campbell, during the early 1990s; the first excerpt is Martens' personal account of the events relating to the death of inmate Robert "Tex" Gentles on October 24, 1993. The prison had been locked down for a couple of days; tension was high. Martens lived on Lower G range and Gentles's cell was on the tier above. The second excerpt is the statement of a Brazilian inmate, Joe Prates, made for the records of the prison violence project. These writings appear to contain some hearsay and imagined dialogue introduced, presumably, to achieve continuity. The special value of these records is that they represent unique first-hand inmate descriptions of events surrounding the death of Robert "Tex" Gentles.

EXCERPT NUMBER ONE:
October 24, Sunday, 9:57 a.m. [1993]
I woke up, disturbed by some noise. Usually Sunday morning was dead quiet, everybody slept till noon, the cells locked except for

those going to yard. Music was playing loud, a serious transgression, something was wrong. Annoyed I sat up in bed and pushed on the barred door. Locked. Very unusual. I heard guys yelling upstairs [on Upper G].

"Where is my breakfast!?" "You have to feed us!"

"Go back to bed, you get nothing!" a guard answered belligerently.

10:15 a.m.

"Guard up! [This is the customary call for assistance.] I need to see the nurse!" I30 [a code meaning Inmate 30 to protect his anonymity], an African American on 1G [range] required emergency medical attention for a cut he gave himself after falling off his bunk onto the concrete floor. He was epileptic, which was a serious hazard, since everything was made of concrete, limestone or steel.

"The nurse doesn't want to see you," G31 [the guard] answered.

"Why?"

"Because she doesn't want to see you."

"Are you prejudiced, Mr. G31?"

"No," he said quietly and walked away. I30 will have to suffer. He could take comfort that the reason for the lack of action was apathy, not racism.

12:30 p.m.

Stereos and prisoners were shrieking at full volume. Cups banged against bars and metal desks smashed into the concrete walls. Cons kicked their metal desks and the iron cell doors throughout the institution. Three cells down from me, I13, the committee man [from the Prison Violence Committee] was playing his superstereo loud, trying to enjoy the lock-down.

Suddenly a goon squad made up of three guards appeared in front of his cell. "We'll force you to turn your radio down!"

"I'd probably get a hundred dollars for that stereo on the street," a male guard said. I13 turned it down, knowing that the guards had been stealing radios out of cells and property stores for years. Not one of them has ever been caught. How do the police police themselves? Six months ago one guard stole a whole welding unit from the metal shop and took it home in full view of everyone. Unfortunately for I10, someone had to account for the missing welder. He was serving a life sentence anyway. No one wondered what an inmate would do with a welder that was wider than his cell.

1:15 p.m.

Finally we were fed. They reluctantly started feeding us when the disturbances threatened to get out of hand. Eight guards were standing in the Dome as our range, Lower G, filed out for the meal. Usually there were only four guards. Their eyes burned into ours as we filed past, looking in each face with intense hostility, trying to intimidate or incite us. The Ass't Warden, Programs, A32, was standing at the door of the servery. I33, my neighbour, and I walked by him.

"Is this lockdown due to the overdoses and the suicides?" I asked, stopping the procession to talk to the Ass't Warden.

"Yes, that and other bad things," he said.

I got my meal and when I came back I stopped by him again. "When do you think we'll get out?" Both of us looked straight ahead at a phalanx of mean guards in the Dome, somehow not daring to take our eyes off them in case they attacked. I felt that he wanted me to keep moving, but he knew that I was on the Prison Violence Committee and had an impact on the prisoners.

"Tomorrow at the latest," he said.

"All right," I said.... I walked into the Dome, keeping an eye on the glowering guards.

1:30 p.m.

I was sitting in my locked cell ... Stereos were still pounding out heavy metal and rap music on Upper G since they had not been fed yet. Suddenly there was a banging coming [through] my ceiling. A serious fight was going on, but obviously somebody was losing badly. A body hit the floor hard and repeatedly. Prisoners were screaming above the blows.

"What are you doing to him?"

"Stop kicking me! I give up!" a strained voice shouted in protest. Then there was silence. Heavy boots hit the stairs in front of my cell, struggling with their load. Four guards were carrying Tex, Robert Wayne Gentles as his mother knew him, down the stairs, his hands and feet hog-tied with his legs and hands handcuffed behind him. A gurgling rattle came from his throat as his head hung limply, almost touching his chest. I've heard that death rattle before. He was either unconscious or dead.

As they came down to the second set of winding stairs, they turned to go down. Tex's head hit the railing, which sounded like a bell being rung.

"Watch his head," one guard said. G34, the female guard, grabbed Tex's hair and pulled his head back. They started their descent down the last flight of stairs. She let go of his hair and his head flopped back down on his chest.

"Tex are you all right?" I19 on 2G called out.

"What's wrong with Tex?" I17 on 2G asked the guards as they carried Tex's body by his cell.

"See what happens when you're disruptive?" G34 spit out. The prisoners in Lower G reacted instinctively. "Go to hell!" "Fuck you, pig!" "If he's dead, you're next!!"

As the morbid procession moved through the final barrier, the last guard smiled and waved at us. "See you later, girls." Smiling and proud of his kill. The cons exploded with fury. Rattling bars and screams of rage. "Fuck you, asshole!" I14 below me yelled. "We'll get you one day, pigs!"

2:30 p.m.
Unit Manager A35 and another management type in a suit came through Upper G barrier and quietly snuck up the first flight of stairs. They stood there looking up the stairs to Upper G and listened, oblivious to the men in Lower G only ten feet from them. Management never came to the area where prisoners lived, in fact most cons would never see a warden or a unit manager for their entire sentence. Thus, the suits had not acquired the knack for looking through wire mesh, stairs, and bars.

Management also did not know they were being observed. They lit cigarettes and smiled, chatting in whispers, excited at their safe little game of "I Spy." Safe in such a murderous environment.... A35 turned to walk down the stairs and flicked his cigarette on the clean floor, an offence that would have warranted a beating if the inmate cleaner had ever caught him.

"How's it going there, Mr. A35?" I said in a calm voice as he passed by my cell. He [was] startled and turned around, not knowing where the sound came from. I stood right in front of him, a wire mesh and bars the only obstacle between us. "Not bad, not bad," he said in a quiet, nervous voice, hurrying out through the barrier [leading to the Dome area].

3:00 p.m.
Cell searches started on Lower G and throughout the joint. I36 in 6 on 1G was taken out and strip-searched in segregation. No drugs or weapons were found. I7 and three other prisoners also had their cells searched. Nothing found. Heavy metal music, militant rap music, and smashing cups reverberated all over the prison.

7:43 p.m.
We finally received our first meal since yesterday afternoon. [The diarist seems confused here. He was fed at 1:15 p.m. earlier that day.] They unlocked our range so that we could walk to the servery to pick up our meal. One tier at a time was being let out for meals. Usually two to four tiers were let out. As I came out of our range and into the Dome, Dr. P37 the psychologist, was standing near the entrance with Unit Manager A35. They were there to gauge our hostility and report back to administration. Walking by the psychologist I looked him in the eye and he turned away quietly.

Eight guards with guns were on the catwalk that ringed the dome. Ten guards in uniform and a plain clothes officer from the Ontario Provincial Police Penitentiary Squad stood in the dome ready to attack. Case Management Officers stood behind the bullet proof Plexiglas [food service wickets] replacing the inmate servers who were also locked down. They kept their eyes lowered as we filed past. Roast beef, chocolate cake, bread, coffee. An unusually good meal.

7:45 p.m.
"You motherfuckers killed him!" I38 had started his lamentation from Upper G. Staff had not yet reported anything to the cons regarding Tex or the lock-down but after twenty years as a caged human, I38 knew exactly what was going on.

"Go lick your nuts!" the guard yelled back.

"AAAAAAArrrrgggggg!" I38 smashed his toilet and cell in a rage. A nervous guard walked on the range to lock us up for supper.

"Is Tex all right?" I8 asked as the guard walked by his cell. "We know nothing," the guard answered. When he left the locked range, the rumours started to fly. The Jamaicans knew from experience that something evil had happened to Tex.

"Hey, you don't kill one of us and get away with it! It doesn't go down like that!" I16, a huge Jamaican, started to let the guards know the score.

8:29 p.m.
Guards were doing walks every half hour instead of on the hour. They were skittish, humble, and would not confirm anything.

"What the hell happened?" I asked a short guard ... as he walked past my cell. "Hey, I'm only the fifth wheel, they don't tell me anything." He meant that they would not tell the prisoners anything. This is a serious head game to be playing with us. We had a right to know, the stonewalling was too much. Strangely, it seemed like they suddenly had no power. They had been unplugged. Management had withdrawn from them and they were on their own. The penitentiary was suddenly a ship alone in a vast ocean.

9:05 p.m.
I38 had been constantly yelling from Upper G for over an hour. "You fucking goof pigs. Come into my cell and I'll give you a go!" ——— and Tex were his friends and they had been killed by the corrections staff within four days of each other.

"Loooong liiiive the Revolution!!" His voice sang out, long and drawn out, over and over.

Upper F was starting to bang on the bars with cups and shook their cell doors out of hungry outrage. Mixed in with the roar was an undercurrent of laughter. Guards were in the dome laughing and bragging about their kill, certain that some action would occur and that they could use their deer rifles.

"Curses on you fucking swine!" I38 let them know where they stood. "I'll kill your grandchildren!! Looong liiiive the REVOLUTION!"

9:16 p.m.
The nurse came on the range again to hand out medication. A friend of Tex asked for a tranquilizer to calm his nerves. "I'm

not giving out anything but regular medication," she said in a very curt voice.

9:31 p.m.
Mr. G39 did the count, counting men in their cages. As he walked by them, they asked for a word or indication of what had happened. "I know nothing." I33 was trying a different tactic. He knew that G39 did not like one of the guards on the goon squad that went after Tex. I33 was trying to use this hate to pry some information about Tex's condition.

9:46 p.m.
The lights went out on Upper F, the power had been turned off due to their caged uprising. From Upper G a lone, wounded voice still drowned out all the others. "Looong liive the Revvvvooolutiooon!"

9:47 p.m.
Prisoners on Upper G started smashing cups and anything metal against metal. Our lights went out as well. No matter. Electricity could not assist us anyway. We were no longer pacified by the idiot box or the crooning from the radio. We wanted to smash everything and we did not need electricity to do that... We had fire and rage, something that always lurked just below the surface and could never be taken away by those in power. Everything they did against us gave us more fuel.

9:57 p.m.
Prisoners from Upper H were calling to us across the service corridor between G block and H block. A narrow service corridor ran behind the two ranges of cells. Four metal walkways were suspended in space behind each tier so that the plumbers could fix broken pipes and the guards could stick rifles through the peep hole at the back of our cells. [Recall that armed guards fired into several cells through these peep holes in the course of quelling the 1932 riot.]

Getting down on my knees below the sink at the back of my cell, I listened through the small wire mesh vent hole [not to be confused with the peep hole]. I heard metal on metal banging and a rebel yell.

"Hey G! What happened to Tex?" Voices sounded hollow as they came through my vent. "The fucking coppers killed him!" I30 called back.

"What?" came a confused reply. I30 tried again slowly so that our fellow prisoners could hear. "*T-h-e c-o-p-p-e-r-s k-i-l-l-e-d h-i-m!*" No one answered for a long time. I thought that maybe he did not understand.

"No shit," came a quiet reply. The con on Upper H stood up and went to the front of his cell to report to his range. We could barely hear their voices, then they exploded in a fit of metal banging and guttural yells of anger.

Our lights just came on again. H block called over again. "So what are you guys doing about it?" "Nothing! We're locked down!" I30 answered. The Jamaicans on our range started to jabber excitedly to each other in pidgin English. Their language came from the days when the English had them enslaved, but they had added their own twist, making it their own. Now they used it to their advantage.

I went to my metal shelf bolted into the concrete wall and pulled down a red shirt. I wanted to wear the blood that was being spilled over me. The power came on again and "We Will Rock You" began playing loud from someone's radio, the bass pounded in rhythm with our rage.

"Long live the revolution! Long memories!" I38 started again upstairs. I23 from the end of the range on two says, "Let's get the Citizens Advisory Committee!"

"Are you kidding?! They're part of security!" someone below answered incredulously. [The Citizens Advisory Committee was not informed of the Gentles incident when it happened. If an outside observer or the senior officer in charge of the prison had been on Upper G range that Sunday, Gentles would have been handled differently].

10:30 p.m.
The nurse came on the range again with medication. The guard walked with her as a protective escort and did a count at the same time.

"Looong liiiive the Reeeevoluuuution! Down with the government!" Angry voices floated from the cages around her. She jumped at the noise and hostility.

"My ancestors fought against hypocrisy and tyranny! I'llllll bring you REVOLUTION!" Prisoners were joining I38 in a mutual exclamation of pain.

"Down with the government! Do you want vengeance!? Do you hear me?!" "YES!!" a chorus answered.

"It's going to happen!" Our committee man I13 blurted excitedly.

"What's going to happen?" someone a few cells down asked.

"REALITY!" I38 screamed from upstairs. "I will fuck you for a thousand years! Long live the revolution! I-WILL-NOT-FORGET! Freedom and democracy not hypocrisy! How dare you!"

"War!" echoes from Upper F across the dome.

My TV flickered in front of me with the sound off. The Blue Jays victory parade marched through Toronto with a big Canada theme [a replay]. Canadian flags were seen everywhere. The Toronto Metro Police were the honour guard for the procession. The manager for the Blue Jays was a Jamaican and wore a jacket displaying his loyalty to the Jamaican colours. Tomorrow the federal election will be held to see who will lead our country. ———'s funeral [the inmate who died three days earlier] will be held on Tuesday.

THE SECOND EXCERPT:

Statement of what I, Joe Prates, saw and heard on Sunday, October 24, 1993, in the Kingston Penitentiary in cell 3-G-10. I am a Brazilian citizen.

I woke up around more or less at 09:00 hours. So I wonder if I miss breakfast or if they will serve it. I ask at the range, "Is there somebody woke?" Couple of guys said yes.

"What's up, Joe?" So I said, "My door is close. I miss breakfast, and I think we are in lock-up for something!"

So I ask my neighbour, cell 11-3-G, the range rep, "What's going on? It's 09:00 and the doors still closed and they didn't serve breakfast."

"I think we are in lock-up. I will check it out," he said to me. So they said we are in lock-up and they will put something on news channel 13. At ten o'clock will start feeding and we are in lock-up for pills, drugs, and weapons.

OK, Tex, that is Robert Gentles, woke around ten o'clock

and he and me was talking about sports, soccer. What's had happened yesterday, Saturday. Brazilian boys playing soccer in Spain. And race car. Another Brazilian boy win in Japan... and I told him we are in lock-up and they will start feeding us at ten o'clock. So ten o'clock pass, ten-thirty pass...eleven o'clock and nothing, nobody came to say something.

We are starting get hungry ... already twenty hours without food. Because last supper was Saturday around four o'clock. More and more guys woke now and hungry and we started asking when they will give some food. And asking for some information, or let the range rep out for some hot water.

But nothing, so we start making noise, banging the doors and yelling and throwing little balls of paper out the window in front of my cell.[The high windows of the cell block were approximately twelve feet across the range from the gates of the cells]. The wind was playing with everything on the range, on the floor. So a little fire start just in front of my cell and the wind bring this in front of Tex's cell. It was one page of newspaper on fire.

"Fuck, man," Tex said. "They are doing fire, amigo. It is not good to do fire, tell them to stop the fucking fire, it's bad." The newspaper that was on fire came to my cell and come in front of cell 11-3-G.

"Fire is not good." Cell 11 said something like Tex said. "Is better stop it." So. It land in front of my cell and finished, burned till there are only ashes.

Ten or fifteen minutes later, three guards come to the range. One have a fire extinguisher, CO2. "You go the Hole, disassociation cells," they said to me.

"I go the Hole for what?" I asked. "You go the Hole because you start fire." "If you have proof and concrete evidence, then I go the Hole right now. But if you don't have, get the fuck out of here!" So they spray the fire extinguisher on top of the ashes ... and spray the fucking thing inside my cell.

"Man, why are you doing that? Why are you spraying this sheet [sic] in my cell?" "It's for your own protection," he said. "I don't need protection like that." I started coughing and they started laughing. They left the range, so I fucking clean my cell floor because I have a lot of this fucking yellow powder in there. I clean it up, it took me at least one hour to clean my cell....

Around one o'clock the guards came back on the range again.

But now it was at least twelve guards. Mr. —— and three guards are just in front of my cell. Miss —— was there too.

"Somebody told me you are black belt in martial arts, is it true?" I asked Mr. ——. "FUCK OFF!" "What you say?" FUCK OFF, PRATES!"

"Thank you very much, officer, because I will put another complaint against you for your violent and abusive language towards me again." The other guard came in front of my cell. "You will be crying today," he said....

They started provoking me, but every time they said something to me, I just said, "Thank you very much, officer." So they stop the mental game with me. I did not play the way they are expecting.

Then they went in front of Tex's cell. "Hey man, it's almost one o'clock and nobody got any food and you guys said lunch will start at ten o'clock," Tex asked. "Why don't you mind your own fucking business?" Mr. —— said to Tex. "It's my business because I'm hungry and it's your job." "Are you trying to tell me how to do my fucking job?!" Mr. —— said to Tex. "I didn't say that, you said that."

Another guard who was standing there started saying, "He had a bad attitude. This guy has a bad attitude." "You can go the Hole for that," Mr. —— told Tex. "I don't see any reason for me to go to the Hole."

They started provoking him. Then there were five guards in front of his cell. One came to me and said "You go back to the back of your cell. Get away from the front of your cell." I wouldn't move from my bars. "I will stay here in the front of my cell."

They opened [Tex's] cell and came inside his cell. I try to talk to him but he didn't answer me no more. For five minutes, six or seven guards were in his cell. When they bring him out he was with irons on his legs, his arms and he look like unconscious. They drop him on the floor. His front on the floor. He was flat on the floor. No sign of life. No movements. I try to talk to him but he didn't answer me.

Miss —— said, "Give him some more!" One said, "No! It's done."

"What you done to him? You kill him, you motherfucker!" I said.

"And you will be next," Mr —— said. "What!?" I started

yelling to the range. "Tex is unconscious on the floor! Like a death, and they said I will be next. If something happen to me, please phone 922-2503, it's the Brazilian embassy!"

Some guys yelled, "Amigo, say the number again!" I told the number for three more times and they drag him away. It was the last time I saw him.

October 27, 1993
[An entry timed 3:16 p.m. describes inmate Prates's experience at the regional treatment centre earlier in the year. According to the entry, he was treated for antisocial behaviour with a drug called chlorpromazine and returned to the main cell block "half insane."]

6:30 p.m.
Joe was carrying his tray of food back to his cell, a black armband around his arm in respect for Tex's memory. "They interview anybody yet, Joe?" a prisoner in a locked cell asked him. "Yeah, a few other guys and me. I told them they killed Tex in the cell and then they threw him out of his cell. I called out to him 'Tex, Tex, are you all right?' but Tex ... he was dead."

November 1, 1993, 10:34 a.m.
Joe was called out to see ———, a psychologist. She wanted to see what condition he was in. He came down the stairs in a bubbly mood and stopped to yell into his friend's cell shouting above the roar of five hundred prisoners. "I have to see the bitch!" he said in a heavy Brazilian accent. "Be careful, amigo!" Jeff warned Joe. Off he went out of the barrier to have his sanity measured....

10:44 a.m.
The escort guard opened the interview door for Joe. Behind a lone government desk sat a red-headed psychologist, ———. She reached down and grabbed her purse, placing it on the table. Joe sat down in the plastic chair as she continued searching for something in the purse. Joe could hear a faint click coming from the leather bag. Finally she brought out a piece of paper and placed it on the table without looking at it... "Are you OK?" she asked. "Fine," he said. "Tex is the one who is not OK."

She ignored the comment.... She asked Joe to repeat what he had seen on October 24, which he did, exactly as he told the police.

"The papers are just turning a regular incident into a major exaggeration," the psychologist said with a wave of her hand. "Why are you putting yourself through all this hardship? Just let it go, we will take care of it."

Joe's sleepless red eyes widened. "Tex was my friend. I can never let it go." She looked at him solemnly, assessing his mental stability. "The guards were just trying to take him to the hole because it was their job. They don't kill people. It was his fault, don't you agree? Didn't Tex do cocaine? It is very unhealthy to lift weights and do drugs."

Joe became more agitated. "Tex didn't do any dope, you know that. I can't believe what I am hearing. Man, you people are cold. Can I have smoke?" She reached into her purse and took a long custom cigarette from a black case. Joe's attitude softened as he inhaled deeply.... He will remember and savour that cigarette for a long time.

"How much time are you doing?" she asked. "Three years," he said luxuriously blowing the smoke at the ceiling. "Wouldn't you rather go back to your homeland, Brazil?" she asked. "No, and I don't agree with your story, either," he answered, smiling. Ice flowed through her veins as she turned off her emotional warmth. "All right, you can leave now."

November 2, 1993 8:30 a.m.
In the prison gym one old guard sat in the gun cage situated in a corner, a shotgun for company. Nobody noticed him today; most of the prisoners were still a bit stunned that another of them went out in a body bag. They tried to work off their energy from the lock-down by lifting weights. Even a few old men were creaking through light weight workouts. Brazilian Joe set down his bar and turned to his friend puffing away beside him. "Hey man, check this out. The Brazilian embassy phoned the warden demanding that I be protected and that the guards who killed Tex be removed from the range. If they hurt me there will be international notice." He picked up his bar, storing up some more strength.

[There is then a description of an aggressive guard with an alleged fondness for guns.]

November 8, 1993 3:00 p.m.

There was an intense discussion in the yard today. A prisoner had found out that a huge weight-lifter named ———— had received two hundred dollars from the guards to seriously hurt Joe Prates. Everyone agreed that ———— should be run off to Protective Custody. But should he go via the hospital? [Convict justice put the weight-lifter at risk of a beating by other prisoners]. That was the question on everyone's mind.

November 9, 1993 11:15 a.m.

Joe Prates stood at the mesh barrier that separated the upper block of cells from the lower block. He was intently studying the *Kingston Whig-Standard*, Canada's oldest newspaper. "Hey, look at this, Jim," he said to the man on the other side of the wire. "'Prison probe doesn't live up to billing. The Correctional Service has backtracked on a promise to find an independent person to chair the inquiry into the death of a black inmate at Kingston Penitentiary. Instead, the three-person team picked to probe the death of Robert Wayne Gentles, 23, of Hamilton, all work for the Correctional Service.'" Joe looked up, amazement on his face. "Can you believe the balls? Man, those people don't give a shit about anybody or any laws."

Joe shook his head and looked back at the paper. He continued, "Mr. ———— [the same guard identified above as Mr. ———— on the afternoon of October 24] is now working Upper G again. I asked him, 'why are you still working?' [He] answered, 'Fuck off.' I said, 'What?' He said, 'Fuck off! I'm going to be on you, you fucking rat!' So I went and phoned the Brazilian embassy, scared for my life. I told them that the guard that killed Tex and had threatened to kill me was back working Upper G. The embassy said that they would get on it."…. "Ah, don't worry so much, Joe. This is 1993, they don't pull that shit, man." "Yeah, tell that to Tex."

12:03 p.m.

The prison goon squad pounded up the metal stairs to Upper G, the same range of cells where they had killed Robert "Tex" Gentles only two weeks before. They pushed and bullied the eight prisoners that were unlocked back into their cells. When all forty men were secured in their cells, they walked over to Joe Prates's cell and stood at his gate waiting for it to buzz open.

"What do you want?" Joe asked from the back of his cell, fear making his voice quaver. "I haven't done anything." "Come out of your cell, you're going to the hole for the good order of the institution," Mr. ———— said, smiling.... "But I haven't done anything. You are going to kill me now. Well, kill me here, not in the Hole," [Joe] said defiantly, looking for something to defend himself with.

The rest of the prisoners were locked down, but they held mirrors through the bars and watched the recurring scene through the reflections. This time they yelled at the top of their lungs. "Are you going to kill another one??! You can't get away with this!"

A guard walked down the range and yanked mirrors from hands, bruising arms on the bars.... "Hey, guys!" Joe yelled as they led him away in handcuffs, "Phone the Brazilian embassy! Hurry before they kill me!"

[The next section of the Prates record is an analysis of the techniques used by prison staff to bring about a change of heart and a recantation from a prisoner detained for a long period in the Hole. It is implied that Prates was kept in a dissociation cell (i.e., the Hole), during the entire winter of 1993–94].

April 20, 1994, 4:30 p.m.
The Kingston Penitentiary was locked down. Two immigration officers took Joe out of the prison, handcuffed and shackled. He has been deported to Brazil. All of the eyewitnesses to the killing of Robert Gentles are now deported or transferred to other prisons. The case is technically lost, but the Gentles family is still fighting for justice.

Author's postscript:
The head of the Prison Violence Project was himself transferred to another prison within a year of the last entry above. The coroner's inquest into the death of Robert "Tex" Gentles continued by fits and starts from the spring of 1998 until June 1999.

APPENDIX C

This is a selection of recommendations from the inquest into the death of Robert Wayne Gentles, an inmate at the Kingston Penitentiary. Gentles died while being extracted from his cell by five guards on October 24, 1993. The inquest was conducted in 1998–99 at Kingston, Ontario, by coroner Benoit Bechard. The entire report may be obtained from the Office of the Chief Coroner, Office of the Attorney General of Ontario, Queen's Park, Toronto, Ontario.

CELL EXTRACTIONS
1. It is recommended that all alternatives be considered before a cell extraction is ordered.

2. ... that all cell extractions be videotaped.

3. ... that all cell extractions of non-compliant inmates except for those in the most extreme situations, such as where actual risk of bodily harm or death may be imminent to any staff or inmate, be conducted by properly trained and equipped Institutional Emergency Response Teams.

4. ... that a fully qualified nurse, doctor, or paramedic be present

during all IERT and non-IERT cell extractions for non-compliant inmates. The attending health care professional must be adequately equipped to handle possible medical emergencies and must perform a health check of the inmate immediately following the restraint and prior to removal.

5. ... that CSC maintain an Institutional Emergency Response Team on 24-hour standby in all medium and maximum security institutions. During lock-downs, the IERT should be on-site.

CHEMICAL AGENTS AND INFLAMMATORY SPRAYS

9. ... that CSC only authorize for use those chemical agents, inflammatory sprays and their constituents which meet Health Canada and Environment Canada standards. All chemical agents and inflammatory sprays in use by CSC must be re-authorized annually.

10. ... that for each individual incident for which chemical agents/inflammatory sprays are to be used they be used only upon the specific authority of the person who is in charge of the institution at that time. This will be done in accordance with the Commissioner's Directives and Standard Operating Procedures. The person in charge must make himself/herself aware of the reason for the request for chemical agent/inflammatory spray before authorizing its use.

11. ... that, when time and circumstances permit, before a chemical agent/inflammatory spray is administered to an inmate that the medical authority at the institution be called to check the inmate's medical file for possible adverse effects to the chemical agents/inflammatory spray. If that is not possible, and when time and circumstances permit, a continually updated list of inmates with medical conditions that might be adversely affected by chemical agents/inflammatory sprays shall be available on each living unit and must be checked.

12. ... that chemical agents/inflammatory sprays continue to be used only by properly trained staff.

LOCKDOWNS

18. ... that during a lockdown adequate meals be served at reasonable intervals. The first meal of the day should be served to all inmates no later than 11:00 a.m.

SEGREGATION

19. ... that when administrative segregation is used, it is used in compliance with institutional procedures and the law and appropriately monitored by senior management.

TRAINING

21. ... that all correctional officers receive refresher training every three years in the following areas:

   — CSC and the law
   — Use of Force Management Model
   — Cell Extraction Procedures
   — Restraint Equipment
   — Arrest and Control
   — Use of Force and
   — Chemical Agents

22. ... that all employees of CSC continue to receive training in anti-racism, cultural awareness and harassment.

26. Recognizing the potential negative impact on correctional officers working in an institutional setting, CSC must continue to train new recruits and existing staff in accordance with the values expressed in the Mission of the Correctional Service of Canada.

29. ... that training be provided in how to lift and carry an inmate.

THE CORRECTIONAL OFFICER AND STRESS

31. ... that CSC evaluate psychological screening as a component of its officer recruitment program.

33. ... that CSC provide a Stress Management course for staff with an option of professional counselling as needed.

POLICY

43. ... that CSC, with cooperation from the Union of Solicitor General Employees, investigate the possibility of rotating staff among institutions on a regular basis in order to have a turnover of the majority of staff at Kingston Penitentiary.

44. ... that there be formal steps to notify families of a death in the institution. Notification must be made in person.

MANAGEMENT ACCOUNTABILITY

51. ... that all persons in the CSC with specific authority who are empowered or required to dispose of complaints, grievances or investigations be able to admit error on the part of or on behalf of the Correctional Service.

52. ... that CSC initiate a national program of statistical collection, analysis and reporting that will reflect the trends in the use of force, segregation, inmate discipline, inmate grievances, officer discipline, and officer grievances. This would provide indicators to the management team of the performance of their institution.

55. ... that the Warden and Deputy Warden at Kingston Penitentiary be left in place for a minimum three-year term. CSC should consider instituting a system of financial incentives for Wardens and Deputy Wardens to stay in their jobs at difficult posts like Kingston Penitentiary.

58. ... that all levels of management be held accountable for their actions or lack of same. Senior managers who are found to be ineffective should be provided with additional training, retrained, demoted, or dismissed.

DISCIPLINE

60. ... that when allegations of excessive force used against an inmate are proven, the staff member involved be dismissed from the Public Service.

64. ... that an officer who uses an unauthorized control hold be disciplined.

CITIZENS ADVISORY COMMITTEE

65. The public accountability of each Citizens Advisory Committee should be strengthened. To achieve this it is recommended that the Regional Deputy Commissioner, at the beginning of each year, take steps to ensure that each CAC in the Region is at optimum levels of strength and performance. Each committee shall be comprised of at least 3 persons and no more than 7 who are reasonably representative of a cross-section of the community. Newspaper advertisements should be used as necessary to recruit new members. A selection committee made up of the head of the institution, the local union president and the chair of the local CAC shall select new members. The participation of the correctional officers is considered essential in the success of the committee's mandate.

66. ... that each CAC prepare an annual report containing a review of the past year's activities, an assessment of the effectiveness of the committee's monitoring of crisis situations where the safety of staff and/or inmates was clearly at risk and a statement of the needs of the committee in order to carry out their duties in the coming year. The report would be submitted to the Regional Deputy Commissioner, the Correctional Investigator, the head of the institution, and to community agencies and individuals involved in public policy relating to community safety and prisoner rehabilitation.

PATHOLOGY

67. ... that in situations involving the application of chemical agents/inflammatory sprays prior to death, blood and tissue samples be screened for concentrations of chemical agent constituents. In cases where the samples are being forwarded to the Centre for Forensic Sciences ... that they be provided in the amounts and containers specified by the Centre.

68. ... that the post-mortem report and, if possible, the police report, be provided to the Centre for Forensic Sciences along with the Case Submission form when the samples are submitted.

KINGSTON PENITENTIARY

69. It is recommended that a review of Kingston Penitentiary be conducted with respect to its appropriate use within the context of the Corrections and Conditional Release Act. This review should be conducted by a committee consisting of representatives from CSC, the Ministry of the Solicitor General [federal], and independent persons from the community.

70. ... that with the issue of accountability a concern, that increased civilian oversight of CSC is required. An independent oversight committee shall be formed by the Ministry of the Solicitor General to conduct a study and report within 12 months to the Justice Committee of the Parliament of Canada. This committee shall determine what type of civilian oversight body should be established and the scope of its powers.

Author's Postscript:

It should not be a surprise that the report of the coroner's jury in the Gentles case moved well beyond the circumstances and events of the death itself. It confirms the view of J. Michael Yates, author of *Line Screw* (1993) that there is not one well-managed institution within the Canadian corrections system. Else why would a jury of citizens examining the death of a prisoner give so much space in their recommendations to system-wide deficiencies and how they might be remedied? The report of Commissioner Madam Justice Louise Arbour (1995) into certain events at the Prison For Women in Kingston was equally wide-ranging. She found that the strip-searching and the manner of confinement of some women offenders by an all-male ERT team from the Kingston Penitentiary in 1994 were symptomatic of a system lacking in public accountability and contemptuous of the law.

The contents of my book, therefore, come to a focus in recommendations 69 and 70 of the coroner's jury. It is a vindication of my work that a modest coroner and a modest jury of five citizens, in the course of inquiring into a tragic and unnecessary death, went straight to the heart of the matter — mismanagement within a system of which the Kingston Penitentiary is a part. The question begged in no. 69 is whether a nineteenth-century prison can have any continuing usefulness in the twenty-first century. It is a question that may be dodged through benign indifference, fudged in an effort to please the competing interests, or, preferably, dealt with in a forthright manner.

I am not terribly sanguine about the latter possibility. But I am hopeful that the quasi-military hierarchy of the correctional service will be replaced in the foreseeable future by more suitable arrangements for improving public safety.

NOTES

1. From the *Penitentiary Houses Act*, Britain, 1779. As excerpted by C.J. Taylor, *Lawful Authority: Readings on the History of Criminal Justice in Canada*, edited by R.C. MacLeod (1988).

2. Norman Johnston. *The Human Cage: A Brief History of Prison Architecture.* New York: Walker and Company, 1973

3. W.G.C. Norman. "A Chapter of Canadian Penal History." M.A. Thesis, 1979. The Archives of Queen's University at Kingston, Ontario.

4. C.J. Taylor. "The Kingston Ontario Penitentiary and Moral Architecture." A chapter in Section 4, *Lawful Authority*.

5. Regulations for the Provincial Penitentiary, 1836 and 1870, Correctional Service of Canada Museum at Kingston, David St. Onge, Curator.

6. Warden's Report, 1847, Queen's Archives.

7. Report of the Commission to Inquire into and Report upon the Conduct, Economy, Discipline and Management of the Provincial Penitentiary. 30 May 1849. George Brown, Secretary. Queen's Archives.

8. *Journals of the Legislative Assembly*, Vol. 8. Province of Canada, 18 January to 30 May 1849, and Appendix 18, 1856.

9. Dennis Curtis and Andrew Graham. *Kingston Penitentiary: The First Hundred and Fifty Years.* Corrections Canada: Ottawa, 1985. pp. 62ff.

10. Warden's Report, 1856, Queen's Archives.

11. Warden's Report, 1858, Queen's Archives.

12. Dana Johnson, Federal Heritage Building Review Office, Report 8932, CSC Museum.

13. Curtis and Graham.

14. Jennifer McKendry. "An Ideal Hospital for the Insane?" *SSAC Bulletin* Vol. 18, March 1993.

15. David St. Onge, Curator, CSC Museum.

16. Punishment Books, Provincial Penitentiary, Queen's Archives.

17. Liberation Books, Provincial Penitentiary 1850s, Queen's Archives.

18. Curtis and Graham, p. 57

19. Regulations under the *Penitentiary Act of 1868*, CSC Museum.

20. Punishment Books, 1880s, Queen's Archives.

21. R.E. Neufeld. "A World Within Itself: Kingston Penitentiary and Foucauldian Panopticism, 1834–1914." M.A. Thesis, Queen's University, 1993. p. 32

22. Warden's Journals, 1889–1910, Queen's Archives.

23. Warden's Letter Book, 1880s, Queen's Archives.

24. Neufeld.

25. J.T.L. James. *A Living Tradition: Penitentiary Chaplaincy.* Ministry of Supply and Services: Ottawa, 1990.

26. *Report of the Royal Commission on Penitentiaries.* Ottawa: King's Printer, 1914.

27. O.C.J. Withrow. *Shackling the Transgressor.* Toronto: T. Nelson and Sons, 1933.

28. Report by the Committee to Advise upon the Revision of the Penitentiary

Regulations, 28 February 1921; O.M. Biggar, W.F. Nickle, and P.M. Draper (members).

29. *Report of the Superintendent of Penitentiaries on Kingston Penitentiary Disturbances 1932.* Ottawa: King's Printer, 1933.

30. *Royal Commission to Investigate the Penal System of Canada.* Justice Joseph Archambault, Chairman. Ottawa, 1938.

31. *The Telescope*, March 1954 and September 1956, Periodicals Section, Law Library, Queen's University, Kingston.

32. Roger Caron. *Go Boy.* Nelson: Don Mills, 1978. p. 133.

33. CSC Oral History Project, *M. Lillis, 1989-0337.* National Archives, Ottawa.

34. A.J. MacLeod. "The Changing Canadian Prison" (speech pamphlet), 1962.

35. Report of the Commission of Inquiry into Certain Disturbances at Kingston Penitentiary During April 1971, J.W. Swackhamer, Chairman, 1973.

36. *Aftermath of 1971 Riot.* (RCMP silent film). National Archives, Ottawa ISN173575.

37. J.T.L. James. *A Living Tradition.*

38. Luc Gosselin. *Prisons in Canada.* Montreal: Black Rose Books, 1982. p. 82.

39. Mark MacGuigan, Chairman. *Report to Parliament of the Sub-Committee on the Penitentiary System in Canada.* Ottawa: Minister Supply and Services, 1977. p. 2.

40. Canada. *Report of the Solicitor General.* Pierre Cadieux, 1988–89. Ottawa: Ministry of Supply and Services. p. 56.

41. Ruth Morris. *Crumbling Walls: Why Prisons Fail.* Oakville: Mosaic Press, 1989. p. 158.

42. *Kingston Whig-Standard*, Nov.23, 1989.

43. CSC Oral History Project.

44. 1995 National Inmate Survey, Final Report, Correctional Service of Canada, 340 Laurier Ave. W., Ottawa K1A 0P9.

45. Correctional Service of Canada, 1996 Staff Survey, Mike Muirhead, Research Branch, CSC, May 1997.

46. Mission of the Correctional Service of Canada, CSC, Ottawa, 1990

47. Edward Greenspan et al. "Discipline and Parole." *Queen's Quarterly*, Vol. 105, No. 1, Spring 1998. p. 9.

48. Anthony Doob. "Should Canada Maintain Its System of Discretionary Release?" A speech given at the annual general meeting of the John Howard Society (Kingston) September 1998.

49. Dennis Kerr. *Drug Strategy Review Policy.* April 1995, Corrections Canada, Ontario Region.

50. 1996 Staff Survey — see 45 above.

51. Dr. John Molot, letter, 11 May, 1994, to head of Health Services, Kingston Penitentiary and presented as evidence in the federal court hearing, Ottawa, June 3 and 4, 1996, *Stephen Brian Kelly vs The Solicitor General, The Commissioner of Corrections and The Warden at K.P.*, Judge W.P. McKeown presiding.

52. Margaret Brady. "Pens and Needles." *Financial Post*, May 16, 1998.

53. Annual Report, Correctional Investigator, Corrections Canada, Ottawa, 1995–96.
54. *Commission of Inquiry into Certain Events at the Prison For Women in Kingston.* The Honourable Louise Arbour, Commissioner, Public Works and Government Services, Ottawa, 1996. p. 191
55. Maeve McMahon, School of Law, Carleton University, Ottawa, at the Ken Bolton Symposium, Windsor, Nov 6–9, 1997.
56. J. Michael Yates. *Line Screw.* Toronto: McClelland & Stewart, 1993. p. 316.
57. *Kingston Whig-Standard*, July 2, 1998.
58. Basic Facts about Corrections in Canada, 1997, CSC, Ottawa.
59. Papio Lappala-Seppala, Regulating the Prison Population in Finland, a paper presented at the international forum, Beyond Prisons, Kingston, March 15–18, 1998.
60. Peter T. Elikann. *The Tough-On-Crime Myth.* New York: Insight Books, 1996.

INDEX

Peter H. Hennessy is a retired educator — teacher of high school history and, latterly, professor of education at Queen's University in Kingston. While principal of the Port Arthur Collegiate (Thunder Bay) in the 1960s, he developed the fixed idea that schools are comparable with prisons, mental institutions, and homes for the aged. They are all designed, he believes, to shape humans into semi-dependent beings for the convenience of society. That is the animating philosophy of his book.

CPSIA information can be obtained at www.ICGtesting.com
Printed in the USA
LVOW05s0021160115

423016LV00010B/105/P

9 781550 023305